Editor

Mary S. Jones, M.A.

Editor in Chief

Karen J. Goldfluss, M.S. Ed.

Cover Artist

Barb Lorseyedi

Imaging

Leonard P. Swierski

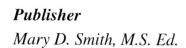

Publisher

Mary D. Smith, M.S. Ed.

Author

Robert W. Smith

Teacher Created Resources, Inc.

12621 Western Avenue

Garden Grove, CA 92841

www.teachercreated.com

ISBN: 978-1-4206-8629-6

©2009 Teacher Created Resources, Inc.

Reprinted, 2017

Made in U.S.A.

Table of Contents

The old adage "practice makes perfect" can really hold true for your child and his or her education. The more practice and exposure your child has with concepts being taught in school, the more success he or she is likely to find. For many parents, knowing how to help your child can be frustrating because the resources may not be readily available and math textbooks can be more confusing than helpful. As a parent it is also difficult to know where to focus your efforts so that the extra practice your child receives at home supports what he or she is learning in school.

This book has been designed to help parents and teachers reinforce basic skills with their children. *Practice Makes Perfect* reviews basic math skills in grade 4. The math focus is on fractions, decimals, and percents. These interrelated concepts are often difficult for even very capable students to grasp. While it would be impossible to include all math concepts taught in grade 4 in this book, the following basic objectives are reinforced through practice exercises arranged in a logical, sequential, and easy-to-use format. These objectives support math standards established on a district, state, or national level. (Refer to the Table of Contents for the specific objectives of each practice page.)

- Equivalent fractions
- Adding and subtracting fractions and decimals
- Converting fractions, decimals, and percents
- Working with mixed numbers and improper fractions
- Computing common denominators
- Comparing and ordering fractions and decimals
- Computing percents
- Reducing fractions
- Operations with money

There are 36 practice pages organized sequentially, so children can build their knowledge from more basic skills to higher-level math skills. (NOTE: Have children show all of their work where computation is necessary to solve a problem.) Following the practice pages are six practice tests. These provide children with multiple-choice test items to help prepare them for standardized tests administered in schools. You may use the fill-in answer sheet on page 46. To correct the test pages and practice pages in this book, use the answer key provided on pages 47 and 48.

How to Make the Most of This Book

Here are some useful ideas for optimizing the practice pages in this book:

- Set aside a specific place in your home to work on the practice pages. Keep it neat and tidy with materials on hand.

- Set up a certain time of day to work on the practice pages. This will establish consistency. An alternative is to look for times in your day or week that are less hectic and are more conducive to practicing skills.

- Keep all practice sessions with your child positive and constructive.

- Help with instructions if necessary. If your child is having difficulty understanding what to do or how to get started, work through the first problem with him or her.

- Review the work your child has done. This serves as reinforcement and provides further practice.

- Allow your child to use whatever writing instruments he or she prefers. For example, colored pencils can add variety and pleasure to drill work.

- Pay attention to the areas in which your child has the most difficulty. Provide extra guidance and exercises in those areas. Allowing children to use drawings and manipulatives, such as coins, tiles, game markers, or flash cards can help them grasp difficult concepts more easily.

- Look for ways to make real-life applications to the skills being reinforced.

Practice 1

Reminder

The **numerator** is the top number in a fraction. It tells the number of parts or sections you are considering.

The **denominator** is the bottom number. It tells the number of parts in the whole set.

Numerator   2   (There are 2 parts you are considering.)

Denominator   3   (There are 3 parts in the whole set.)

Directions: Circle the numerator in each fraction.

1. $\frac{1}{2}$ 2. $\frac{3}{4}$ 3. $\frac{5}{7}$ 4. $\frac{8}{12}$

5. $\frac{6}{11}$ 6. $\frac{7}{23}$ 7. $\frac{9}{10}$ 8. $\frac{7}{13}$

Directions: Draw a box around the denominator in each fraction.

9. $\frac{8}{12}$ 10. $\frac{4}{5}$ 11. $\frac{7}{16}$ 12. $\frac{4}{8}$

13. $\frac{5}{7}$ 14. $\frac{12}{13}$ 15. $\frac{7}{13}$ 16. $\frac{1}{10}$

Directions: Shade in the number of parts represented by the numerator in each fraction.

17. $\frac{2}{3}$ 18. $\frac{4}{5}$ 19. $\frac{7}{8}$ 20. $\frac{1}{8}$

 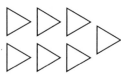 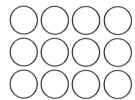

21. $\frac{1}{3}$ 22. $\frac{3}{4}$ 23. $\frac{5}{7}$ 24. $\frac{8}{12}$

 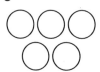  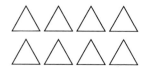

25. $\frac{1}{9}$ 26. $\frac{4}{4}$ 27. $\frac{5}{5}$ 28. $\frac{3}{3}$

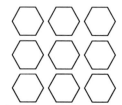  

Practice 2

Directions: Tell how many parts each figure is divided into. Write your answer next to each shape.

1.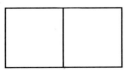

2.

3.

4.

5.

6.

Directions: Write a fraction for the **shaded** part of each figure below. Write your answer next to each shape.

7.

8.

9.

10.

11.

12.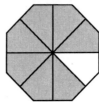

Directions: Name the fraction that tells how much of each figure is **not shaded**. Write your answer next to each shape.

13.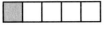

14.

15.

16.

17.

18.

Directions: On the figures below, shade in the amount named by each fraction.

19. $\frac{1}{3}$

20. $\frac{4}{5}$

21. $\frac{4}{9}$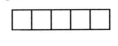

22. $\frac{4}{6}$

23. $\frac{7}{10}$

24. $\frac{5}{8}$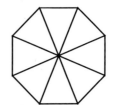

Practice 3

Reminder

Equivalent fractions represent equal amounts divided into a different number of pieces. Equivalent fractions are equal to each other.

The illustration shows that $\frac{2}{2}$ is equal to $\frac{4}{4}$ and that both are equal to 1.

Directions: Name the equivalent fractions represented in the illustrations below. Note that all these equivalent fractions are less than 1. Write the missing numerators and shade in the fraction bars to match. The first two are done for you.

1. $\frac{1}{2} = \frac{2}{4}$

2. $\frac{1}{3} = \frac{2}{6}$

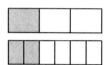

3. $\frac{1}{4} = \frac{}{8}$

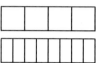

4. $\frac{1}{3} = \frac{}{9}$

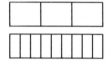

5. $\frac{1}{2} = \frac{}{8}$

6. $\frac{1}{5} = \frac{}{10}$

7. $\frac{3}{4} = \frac{}{8}$

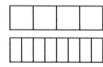

8. $\frac{1}{2} = \frac{}{12}$

9. $\frac{2}{3} = \frac{}{6}$

10. $\frac{1}{4} = \frac{}{12}$

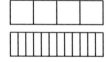

11. $\frac{1}{2} = \frac{}{10}$

12. $\frac{2}{3} = \frac{}{9}$

13. $\frac{}{6} = \frac{2}{3}$

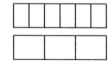

14. $\frac{}{8} = \frac{3}{4}$

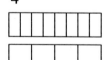

15. $\frac{}{4} = \frac{3}{12}$

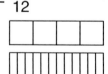

16. $\frac{}{4} = \frac{9}{12}$

17. $\frac{2}{3} = \frac{}{12}$

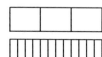

18. $\frac{8}{10} = \frac{}{5}$

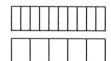

Practice 4

Reminder

Equivalent fractions represent equal amounts divided into a different number of pieces. Equivalent fractions are equal to each other.

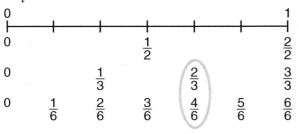

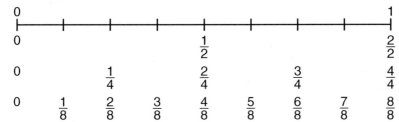

Example:

$$\frac{2}{3} = \frac{4}{6}$$

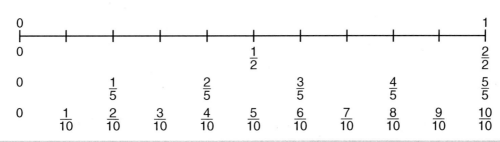

Directions: Use the number lines to determine the equivalent fractions listed below.

1. $\frac{1}{2} = \frac{}{8}$

2. $\frac{1}{4} = \frac{}{8}$

3. $\frac{1}{2} = \frac{}{4}$

4. $\frac{1}{3} = \frac{}{6}$

5. $\frac{2}{3} = \frac{}{6}$

6. $\frac{1}{5} = \frac{}{10}$

7. $\frac{2}{4} = \frac{}{8}$

8. $\frac{3}{4} = \frac{}{8}$

9. $\frac{2}{5} = \frac{}{10}$

10. $\frac{4}{8} = \frac{}{4}$

11. $\frac{4}{8} = \frac{}{2}$

12. $\frac{2}{6} = \frac{}{3}$

13. $\frac{2}{2} = \frac{}{4}$

14. $\frac{3}{3} = \frac{}{6}$

15. $\frac{5}{5} = \frac{}{10}$

16. $\frac{4}{5} = \frac{}{10}$

17. $\frac{3}{5} = \frac{}{10}$

18. $\frac{6}{8} = \frac{}{4}$

19. $\frac{4}{6} = \frac{}{3}$

20. $\frac{6}{8} = \frac{}{4}$

21. $\frac{8}{10} = \frac{}{5}$

22. $\frac{1}{2} = \frac{}{10}$

23. $\frac{1}{2} = \frac{}{6}$

24. $\frac{}{4} = \frac{1}{2}$

25. $\frac{2}{2} = \frac{}{8}$

Practice 5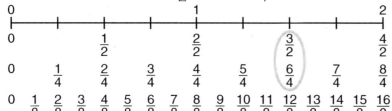

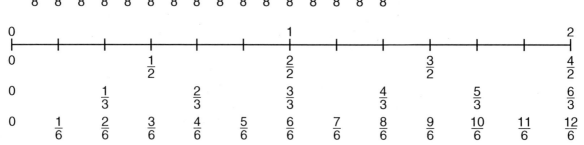

Reminder

Equivalent fractions are equal to each other. Equivalent fractions may be less than or greater than 1. The first number line shows that $\frac{3}{2}$ is equal to $\frac{6}{4}$.

Directions: Use the number lines to determine the equivalent fractions listed below.

1. $\frac{3}{2} = \frac{}{8}$

2. $\frac{5}{4} = \frac{}{8}$

3. $\frac{1}{2} = \frac{}{8}$

4. $\frac{4}{3} = \frac{}{6}$

5. $\frac{5}{3} = \frac{}{6}$

6. $\frac{4}{6} = \frac{}{3}$

7. $\frac{4}{4} = \frac{}{8}$

8. $\frac{3}{3} = \frac{}{6}$

9. $\frac{2}{2} = \frac{}{4}$

10. $\frac{10}{8} = \frac{}{4}$

11. $\frac{16}{8} = \frac{}{4}$

12. $\frac{6}{3} = \frac{}{2}$

13. $\frac{4}{2} = \frac{}{8}$

14. $\frac{3}{4} = \frac{}{8}$

15. $\frac{2}{6} = \frac{}{3}$

16. $\frac{8}{8} = \frac{}{6}$

17. $\frac{3}{2} = \frac{}{6}$

18. $\frac{14}{8} = \frac{}{4}$

19. $\frac{8}{6} = \frac{}{3}$

20. $\frac{10}{8} = \frac{}{4}$

21. $\frac{6}{3} = \frac{}{6}$

22. $\frac{4}{2} = \frac{}{6}$

23. $\frac{4}{2} = \frac{}{4}$

24. $\frac{7}{4} = \frac{}{8}$

25. $\frac{2}{8} = \frac{}{4}$

Practice 6

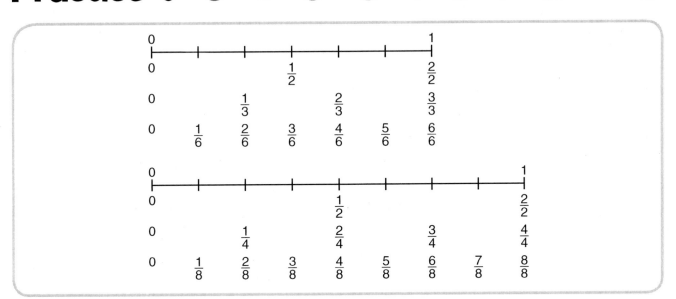

Directions: Use the number lines to help you compare the fraction pairs shown here.
Use > (greater than), < (less than), or = (equal to) to compare each pair.

1. $\dfrac{1}{2}$ _____ $\dfrac{3}{4}$ 2. $\dfrac{5}{8}$ _____ $\dfrac{1}{2}$ 3. $\dfrac{3}{6}$ _____ $\dfrac{1}{3}$ 4. $\dfrac{4}{6}$ _____ $\dfrac{2}{3}$ 5. $\dfrac{7}{8}$ _____ $\dfrac{3}{4}$

6. $\dfrac{1}{8}$ _____ $\dfrac{1}{4}$ 7. $\dfrac{1}{4}$ _____ $\dfrac{3}{8}$ 8. $\dfrac{5}{6}$ _____ $\dfrac{1}{2}$ 9. $\dfrac{4}{4}$ _____ $\dfrac{5}{8}$ 10. $\dfrac{1}{3}$ _____ $\dfrac{5}{6}$

11. $\dfrac{1}{2}$ _____ $\dfrac{1}{3}$ 12. $\dfrac{4}{4}$ _____ $\dfrac{7}{8}$ 13. $\dfrac{1}{3}$ _____ $\dfrac{2}{6}$ 14. $\dfrac{3}{8}$ _____ $\dfrac{2}{4}$ 15. $\dfrac{8}{8}$ _____ $\dfrac{3}{4}$

16. $\dfrac{3}{6}$ _____ $\dfrac{5}{8}$ 17. $\dfrac{4}{8}$ _____ $\dfrac{3}{6}$ 18. $\dfrac{5}{8}$ _____ $\dfrac{3}{4}$ 19. $\dfrac{4}{8}$ _____ $\dfrac{3}{4}$ 20. $\dfrac{3}{6}$ _____ $\dfrac{2}{3}$

21. $\dfrac{5}{6}$ _____ $\dfrac{3}{3}$ 22. $\dfrac{4}{4}$ _____ $\dfrac{5}{6}$ 23. $\dfrac{1}{8}$ _____ $\dfrac{1}{3}$ 24. $\dfrac{1}{4}$ _____ $\dfrac{2}{8}$ 25. $\dfrac{1}{6}$ _____ $\dfrac{1}{2}$

26. $\dfrac{4}{6}$ _____ $\dfrac{4}{8}$ 27. $\dfrac{1}{4}$ _____ $\dfrac{1}{3}$ 28. $\dfrac{1}{3}$ _____ $\dfrac{3}{6}$ 29. $\dfrac{1}{3}$ _____ $\dfrac{2}{8}$ 30. $\dfrac{1}{2}$ _____ $\dfrac{5}{8}$

Practice 7 ❂ ❂ ❂ ❂ ❂ ❂ ❂ ❂ ❂ ❂ ❂

Reminder

- Fractions are in their lowest terms when no factor greater than 1 will divide evenly into both the numerator and the denominator.
- These fractions are in their lowest terms: $\frac{1}{3}, \frac{2}{5}, \frac{5}{7}, \frac{4}{9}, \frac{3}{4}$.
- All fractions with 1 as the numerator and all fractions where the numerator is 1 less than the denominator are in lowest terms: $\frac{1}{4}, \frac{2}{3}, \frac{1}{7}, \frac{4}{5}$.
- Fractions can be reduced to lowest terms by dividing the numerator and denominator by the greatest common factor: $\frac{2 \div 2}{4 \div 2} = \frac{1}{2}$ $\frac{2}{4} = \frac{1}{2}$ (lowest terms)   factors of 2: 1, 2

    factors of 4: 1, 2, 4

Directions: Reduce each fraction to lowest terms. The first two are done for you.

1. $\frac{3 \div 3}{9 \div 3} = \frac{1}{3}$

2. $\frac{10 \div 5}{15 \div 5} = \frac{2}{3}$

3. $\frac{16 \div 4}{20 \div 4} =$

4. $\frac{6}{8} =$

5. $\frac{9}{12} =$

6. $\frac{4}{8} =$

7. $\frac{4}{6} =$

8. $\frac{3}{12} =$

9. $\frac{4}{12} =$

10. $\frac{7}{21} =$

11. $\frac{10}{25} =$

12. $\frac{9}{15} =$

13. $\frac{8}{10} =$

14. $\frac{12}{16} =$

15. $\frac{14}{21} =$

16. $\frac{24}{28} =$

17. $\frac{21}{28} =$

18. $\frac{14}{16} =$

19. $\frac{9}{21} =$

20. $\frac{20}{25} =$

21. $\frac{16}{40} =$

22. $\frac{13}{26} =$

23. $\frac{12}{36} =$

24. $\frac{12}{18} =$

25. $\frac{20}{28} =$

26. $\frac{18}{27} =$

27. $\frac{4}{22} =$

Practice 8

Reminder

When adding fractions with common denominators, add the numerators and keep the denominator the same.

$$\frac{1}{8} + \frac{4}{8} = \frac{5}{8} \qquad \frac{2}{3} + \frac{1}{3} = \frac{3}{3} = 1 \qquad \frac{1}{4} + \frac{2}{4} = \frac{3}{4}$$

Directions: Add these fractions. The first two are done for you.

1. $\frac{3}{10} + \frac{6}{10} = \frac{9}{10}$

2. $\frac{5}{9} + \frac{2}{9} = \frac{7}{9}$

3. $\frac{6}{12} + \frac{5}{12} =$

4. $\frac{3}{6} + \frac{2}{6} =$

5. $\frac{1}{5} + \frac{2}{5} =$

6. $\frac{1}{3} + \frac{1}{3} =$

7. $\frac{4}{9} + \frac{4}{9} =$

8. $\frac{3}{7} + \frac{2}{7} =$

9. $\frac{1}{6} + \frac{4}{6} =$

Directions: Add these fractions. Reduce to lowest terms. The first two are done for you.

10. $\frac{2}{6} + \frac{2}{6} = \frac{4}{6} = \frac{2}{3}$

11. $\frac{1}{2} + \frac{1}{2} = \frac{2}{2} = 1$

12. $\frac{3}{6} + \frac{3}{6} =$

13. $\frac{7}{10} + \frac{2}{10} =$

14. $\frac{2}{5} + \frac{3}{5} =$

15. $\frac{4}{12} + \frac{6}{12} =$

16. $\frac{2}{9} + \frac{1}{9} =$

17. $\frac{5}{7} + \frac{2}{7} =$

18. $\frac{3}{11} + \frac{7}{11} =$

19. $\frac{5}{11} + \frac{5}{11} =$

20. $\frac{7}{12} + \frac{4}{12} =$

21. $\frac{14}{20} + \frac{4}{20} =$

22. $\frac{7}{15} + \frac{6}{15} =$

23. $\frac{8}{9} + \frac{1}{9} =$

24. $\frac{6}{9} + \frac{3}{9} =$

25. $\frac{3}{4} + \frac{1}{4} =$

26. $\frac{6}{11} + \frac{2}{11} =$

27. $\frac{4}{5} + \frac{1}{5} =$

28. $\frac{1}{6} + \frac{2}{6} =$

29. $\frac{3}{9} + \frac{3}{9} =$

30. $\frac{7}{12} + \frac{2}{12} =$

Practice 9 🐚 🐚 🐚 🐚 🐚 🐚 🐚 🐚 🐚 🐚

Reminder

When subtracting fractions with common denominators, subtract the numerators and keep the denominator the same.

$$\frac{5}{8} - \frac{2}{8} = \frac{3}{8} \qquad \frac{7}{10} - \frac{3}{10} = \frac{4}{10} = \frac{2}{5} \qquad \frac{9}{12} - \frac{4}{12} = \frac{5}{12}$$

Directions: Subtract these fractions. Reduce to lowest terms, if necessary. The first two are done for you.

1. $\frac{7}{9} - \frac{3}{9} = \frac{4}{9}$

2. $\frac{6}{8} - \frac{4}{8} = \frac{2}{8} = \frac{1}{4}$

3. $\frac{5}{7} - \frac{3}{7} =$

4. $\frac{6}{6} - \frac{5}{6} =$

5. $\frac{4}{5} - \frac{2}{5} =$

6. $\frac{5}{7} - \frac{1}{7} =$

7. $\frac{5}{9} - \frac{4}{9} =$

8. $\frac{3}{8} - \frac{2}{8} =$

9. $\frac{11}{12} - \frac{5}{12} =$

10. $\frac{6}{9} - \frac{4}{9} =$

11. $\frac{9}{15} - \frac{6}{15} =$

12. $\frac{6}{13} - \frac{4}{13} =$

13. $\frac{7}{10} - \frac{4}{10} =$

14. $\frac{4}{6} - \frac{3}{6} =$

15. $\frac{9}{12} - \frac{6}{12} =$

16. $\frac{5}{7} - \frac{1}{7} =$

17. $\frac{8}{9} - \frac{2}{9} =$

18. $\frac{13}{15} - \frac{7}{15} =$

19. $\frac{5}{10} - \frac{2}{10} =$

20. $\frac{9}{12} - \frac{5}{12} =$

21. $\frac{14}{16} - \frac{4}{16} =$

22. $\frac{9}{10} - \frac{4}{10} =$

23. $\frac{8}{9} - \frac{5}{9} =$

24. $\frac{6}{8} - \frac{2}{8} =$

25. $\frac{7}{11} - \frac{4}{11} =$

26. $\frac{4}{12} - \frac{2}{12} =$

27. $\frac{14}{15} - \frac{11}{15} =$

Practice 10

Directions: Circle the proper fractions below. Draw an X through the improper fractions. Draw a box around the mixed numbers.

1. $\frac{2}{3}$

2. $\frac{6}{5}$

3. $1\frac{1}{3}$

4. $\frac{7}{8}$

5. $\frac{8}{5}$

6. $1\frac{3}{5}$

7. $\frac{4}{9}$

8. $\frac{5}{13}$

9. $\frac{13}{4}$

10. $\frac{6}{6}$

11. $\frac{4}{5}$

12. $2\frac{3}{4}$

13. $\frac{7}{4}$

14. $\frac{8}{4}$

15. $\frac{11}{3}$

16. $1\frac{6}{11}$

17. $\frac{8}{2}$

18. $\frac{13}{12}$

19. $2\frac{3}{7}$

20. $\frac{16}{4}$

21. $\frac{1}{2}$

22. $4\frac{1}{4}$

23. $\frac{17}{4}$

24. $\frac{15}{16}$

25. $\frac{9}{10}$

26. $\frac{10}{9}$

27. $\frac{10}{10}$

28. $1\frac{5}{15}$

29. $5\frac{1}{4}$

30. $\frac{25}{25}$

31. $3\frac{1}{3}$

32. $\frac{9}{3}$

Practice 11

Reminder

Improper fractions are converted into mixed numbers by dividing the numerator by the denominator. The remainder you get after dividing becomes the numerator in the mixed number and the denominator is the same denominator that you started with.

Examples: $\frac{9}{8} = 9 \div 8 = 1\frac{1}{8}$ $\frac{4}{3} = 4 \div 3 = 1\frac{1}{3}$ $\frac{8}{3} = 8 \div 3 = 2\frac{2}{3}$

Directions: Convert these improper fractions to mixed numbers. The first two are done for you.

1. $\frac{9}{5} = 9 \div 5 = 1\frac{4}{5}$

2. $\frac{3}{2} = 3 \div 2 = 1\frac{1}{2}$

3. $\frac{5}{3} = 5 \div 3 =$

4. $\frac{7}{2} =$

5. $\frac{7}{3} =$

6. $\frac{9}{7} =$

7. $\frac{12}{7} =$

8. $\frac{10}{3} =$

9. $\frac{14}{5} =$

10. $\frac{13}{10} =$

11. $\frac{7}{4} =$

12. $\frac{11}{4} =$

13. $\frac{16}{9} =$

14. $\frac{12}{11} =$

15. $\frac{9}{8} =$

16. $\frac{14}{6} =$

17. $\frac{16}{5} =$

18. $\frac{21}{5} =$

19. $\frac{25}{8} =$

20. $\frac{13}{7} =$

21. $\frac{24}{9} =$

22. $\frac{9}{4} =$

23. $\frac{13}{6} =$

24. $\frac{18}{4} =$

25. $\frac{17}{4} =$

26. $\frac{27}{10} =$

27. $\frac{12}{5} =$

28. $\frac{11}{9} =$

29. $\frac{15}{11} =$

30. $\frac{44}{15} =$

31. $\frac{9}{2} =$

32. $\frac{25}{6} =$

33. $\frac{17}{5} =$

Practice 12

Reminder

Mixed numbers are converted into improper fractions by multiplying the denominator times the whole number and adding the numerator. This number becomes the numerator in the improper fraction. The denominator in the improper fraction is the same denominator that you started with in the mixed number.

Examples: $2\frac{1}{3} = (3 \times 2) + 1 = \frac{7}{3}$ $5\frac{3}{4} = (4 \times 5) + 3 = \frac{23}{4}$

Directions: Change these mixed numbers to improper fractions. The first two are done for you.

1. $2\frac{3}{7} =$
$(7 \times 2) + 3 = \frac{17}{7}$

2. $3\frac{1}{2} =$
$(2 \times 3) + 1 = \frac{7}{2}$

3. $5\frac{2}{3} =$

4. $5\frac{1}{2} =$

5. $2\frac{2}{3} =$

6. $4\frac{1}{3} =$

7. $1\frac{2}{7} =$

8. $1\frac{1}{3} =$

9. $1\frac{4}{7} =$

10. $1\frac{3}{8} =$

11. $1\frac{1}{4} =$

12. $3\frac{3}{5} =$

13. $2\frac{1}{5} =$

14. $1\frac{2}{7} =$

15. $4\frac{3}{8} =$

16. $1\frac{2}{8} =$

17. $2\frac{3}{5} =$

18. $2\frac{3}{4} =$

19. $2\frac{7}{8} =$

20. $1\frac{4}{11} =$

21. $2\frac{3}{9} =$

22. $3\frac{1}{3} =$

23. $4\frac{1}{6} =$

24. $5\frac{1}{4} =$

25. $3\frac{2}{6} =$

26. $2\frac{1}{10} =$

27. $1\frac{9}{11} =$

28. $3\frac{3}{8} =$

29. $3\frac{5}{6} =$

30. $4\frac{1}{10} =$

Practice 13

Reminder

You can add mixed numbers by adding the whole numbers and then adding the fractions.

Example: $1\frac{1}{4} + 2\frac{2}{4} = 3\frac{3}{4}$

You may need to reduce the fractions to simplest terms.

Example: $2\frac{1}{3} + 2\frac{2}{3} = 4\frac{3}{3} = 4 + 1 = 5$

Directions: Add or subtract these mixed numbers. Reduce the fractions to simplest terms. The first two are done for you.

1. $1\frac{1}{4}$
   $+ 3\frac{1}{4}$
   $\overline{4\frac{2}{4} = 4\frac{1}{2}}$

2. $4\frac{3}{3}$
   $- 2\frac{1}{3}$
   $\overline{2\frac{2}{3}}$

3. $7\frac{4}{5}$
   $- 2\frac{3}{5}$

4. $3\frac{5}{6}$
   $- 1\frac{4}{6}$

5. $6\frac{3}{4}$
   $- 3\frac{2}{4}$

6. $9\frac{7}{12}$
   $+ 2\frac{4}{12}$

7. $4\frac{2}{6}$
   $+ 3\frac{2}{6}$

8. $5\frac{8}{10}$
   $- 2\frac{7}{10}$

9. $3\frac{4}{5}$
   $- 2\frac{3}{5}$

10. $7\frac{5}{6}$
    $- 3\frac{4}{6}$

11. $6\frac{2}{3}$
    $- 3\frac{1}{3}$

12. $9\frac{3}{4}$
    $- 6\frac{1}{4}$

13. $6\frac{3}{6}$
    $+ 2\frac{1}{6}$

14. $10\frac{1}{3}$
    $+ 5\frac{2}{3}$

15. $2\frac{1}{5}$
    $- 1\frac{1}{5}$

16. $4\frac{7}{10}$
    $+ 2\frac{3}{10}$

17. $4\frac{2}{7}$
    $- 1\frac{2}{7}$

18. $3\frac{7}{12}$
    $+ 2\frac{5}{12}$

19. $5\frac{4}{13}$
    $+ 2\frac{9}{13}$

20. $4\frac{3}{4}$
    $+ 2\frac{1}{4}$

21. $8\frac{4}{8}$
    $- 2\frac{1}{8}$

22. $7\frac{3}{11}$
    $- 4\frac{3}{11}$

23. $5\frac{7}{8}$
    $+ 2\frac{1}{8}$

24. $7\frac{3}{4}$
    $- 2\frac{2}{4}$

25. $8\frac{4}{7}$
    $- 1\frac{3}{7}$

Practice 14 ✿ ᦔ ✿ ✿ ᦔ ✿ ᦔ ✿ ᦔ ✿

Reminder

To compute a common denominator for fractions, you first need to find the least common multiple (LCM) of the two denominators.

To get the lowest common denominator for $\frac{1}{2}$ and $\frac{3}{5}$, find the LCM of 2 and 5.

- multiples of 2: 2, 4, 6, 8, 10, 12 …
- multiples of 5: 5, 10, 15 …

10 is the LCM

Multiply the numerator by the same number you multiplied the denominator in order to get the LCM.

$$\frac{1 \times 5}{2 \times 5} = \frac{5}{10} \qquad \frac{3 \times 2}{5 \times 2} = \frac{6}{10}$$

Directions: Compute the lowest common denominator for each set of fractions. Convert each fraction to the common denominator. The first two are done for you.

1. $\frac{2}{3} = \frac{\times 2}{\times 2} = \frac{4}{6}$

   $\frac{1}{2} = \frac{\times 3}{\times 3} = \frac{3}{6}$

2. $\frac{3}{4} = \frac{\times 5}{\times 5} = \frac{15}{20}$

   $\frac{4}{5} = \frac{\times 4}{\times 4} = \frac{16}{20}$

3. $\frac{1}{2} =$

   $\frac{1}{7} =$

4. $\frac{4}{5} =$

   $\frac{3}{3} =$

5. $\frac{3}{6} =$

   $\frac{1}{4} =$

6. $\frac{5}{8} =$

   $\frac{1}{3} =$

7. $\frac{4}{5} =$

   $\frac{1}{7} =$

8. $\frac{2}{3} =$

   $\frac{1}{4} =$

9. $\frac{1}{7} =$

   $\frac{2}{3} =$

10. $\frac{1}{3} =$

    $\frac{1}{2} =$

11. $\frac{1}{5} =$

    $\frac{2}{4} =$

12. $\frac{1}{5} =$

    $\frac{1}{6} =$

13. $\frac{1}{8} =$

    $\frac{1}{3} =$

14. $\frac{3}{4} =$

    $\frac{1}{7} =$

15. $\frac{1}{6} =$

    $\frac{2}{7} =$

16. $\frac{1}{9} =$

    $\frac{2}{4} =$

17. $\frac{3}{5} =$

    $\frac{3}{9} =$

18. $\frac{1}{10} =$

    $\frac{1}{4} =$

Practice 15 ✺ ➷ ✺ ✺ ➷ ✺ ➷ ✺ ➷ ✺

Reminder

To compare fractions with unlike denominators, you first need to compute the common denominator by finding the least common multiple (LCM) of the two denominators.

To get the lowest common denominator for $\frac{1}{3}$ and $\frac{3}{4}$, find the LCM of 3 and 4.

- multiples of 3: 3, 6, 9, 12, 15 . . .
- multiples of 4: 4, 8, 12, 16 . . .

12 is the LCM

Multiply the numerator by the same number you multiplied the denominator in order to get the LCM.

Now compare the numerators. 4 is less than 9, so $\frac{4}{12}$ is less than $\frac{9}{12}$. That means $\frac{1}{3}$ is less than $\frac{3}{4}$.

$$\frac{1 \times 4}{3 \times 4} = \frac{4}{12} \qquad \frac{3 \times 3}{4 \times 3} = \frac{9}{12}$$

Directions: Use > (greater than), < (less than), or = (equal to) to compare each set of fractions below after computing the lowest common denominator. The first two are done for you.

1. $\frac{1}{2}$ __>__ $\frac{2}{5}$

$\frac{1}{2} = \frac{\times 5}{\times 5} = \frac{5}{10}$

$\frac{2}{5} = \frac{\times 2}{\times 2} = \frac{4}{10}$

2. $\frac{2}{4}$ __<__ $\frac{3}{5}$

$\frac{2}{4} = \frac{\times 5}{\times 5} = \frac{10}{20}$

$\frac{3}{5} = \frac{\times 4}{\times 4} = \frac{12}{20}$

3. $\frac{3}{8}$ _____ $\frac{2}{4}$

4. $\frac{3}{4}$ _____ $\frac{6}{8}$

5. $\frac{5}{6}$ _____ $\frac{2}{3}$

6. $\frac{4}{8}$ _____ $\frac{1}{2}$

7. $\frac{3}{5}$ _____ $\frac{2}{4}$

8. $\frac{4}{9}$ _____ $\frac{1}{2}$

9. $\frac{3}{7}$ _____ $\frac{1}{2}$

10. $\frac{5}{8}$ _____ $\frac{2}{3}$

11. $\frac{1}{3}$ _____ $\frac{2}{6}$

12. $\frac{4}{12}$ _____ $\frac{1}{4}$

13. $\frac{3}{10}$ _____ $\frac{1}{3}$

14. $\frac{2}{3}$ _____ $\frac{3}{4}$

15. $\frac{3}{4}$ _____ $\frac{9}{12}$

16. $\frac{1}{5}$ _____ $\frac{3}{10}$

17. $\frac{5}{6}$ _____ $\frac{9}{10}$

18. $\frac{4}{8}$ _____ $\frac{5}{10}$

Practice 16

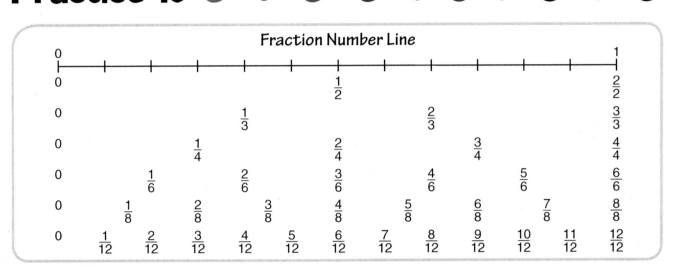

Directions: Use the number line to help you order these proper fractions from **least to greatest**. The first one is done for you.

1. $\frac{3}{4}$ ___ $\frac{4}{12}$
    $\frac{4}{12}$ ___ $\frac{1}{2}$
    $\frac{1}{2}$ ___ $\frac{3}{4}$

2. $\frac{4}{6}$ ___
    $\frac{1}{2}$ ___
    $\frac{5}{12}$ ___

3. $\frac{2}{6}$ ___
    $\frac{1}{2}$ ___
    $\frac{2}{3}$ ___

4. $\frac{5}{6}$ ___
    $\frac{2}{3}$ ___
    $\frac{1}{2}$ ___

5. $\frac{7}{12}$ ___
    $\frac{1}{2}$ ___
    $\frac{2}{6}$ ___

6. $\frac{4}{12}$ ___
    $\frac{1}{2}$ ___
    $\frac{1}{6}$ ___

7. $\frac{2}{8}$ ___
    $\frac{1}{6}$ ___
    $\frac{1}{2}$ ___

8. $\frac{8}{12}$ ___
    $\frac{3}{6}$ ___
    $\frac{1}{4}$ ___

9. $\frac{2}{3}$ ___
    $\frac{5}{6}$ ___
    $\frac{1}{2}$ ___

10. $\frac{1}{2}$ ___
    $\frac{1}{3}$ ___
    $\frac{1}{6}$ ___

11. $\frac{5}{12}$ ___
    $\frac{1}{3}$ ___
    $\frac{1}{2}$ ___

12. $\frac{3}{8}$ ___
    $\frac{6}{12}$ ___
    $\frac{2}{3}$ ___

13. $\frac{1}{4}$ ___
    $\frac{1}{3}$ ___
    $\frac{1}{8}$ ___

14. $\frac{2}{3}$ ___
    $\frac{2}{6}$ ___
    $\frac{2}{4}$ ___

15. $\frac{4}{8}$ ___
    $\frac{4}{6}$ ___
    $\frac{3}{4}$ ___

16. $\frac{7}{8}$ ___
    $\frac{10}{12}$ ___
    $\frac{3}{4}$ ___

17. $\frac{1}{12}$ ___
    $\frac{1}{8}$ ___
    $\frac{1}{6}$ ___

18. $\frac{5}{8}$ ___
    $\frac{9}{12}$ ___
    $\frac{1}{2}$ ___

19. $\frac{3}{6}$ ___
    $\frac{9}{12}$ ___
    $\frac{1}{4}$ ___

20. $\frac{5}{6}$ ___
    $\frac{5}{12}$ ___
    $\frac{5}{8}$ ___

21. $\frac{4}{6}$ ___
    $\frac{3}{4}$ ___
    $\frac{10}{12}$ ___

22. $\frac{3}{12}$ ___
    $\frac{1}{6}$ ___
    $\frac{3}{4}$ ___

23. $\frac{5}{8}$ ___
    $\frac{5}{6}$ ___
    $\frac{1}{2}$ ___

24. $\frac{11}{12}$ ___
    $\frac{3}{4}$ ___
    $\frac{5}{6}$ ___

25. $\frac{1}{2}$ ___
    $\frac{2}{12}$ ___
    $\frac{6}{8}$ ___

Practice 17 ✺ ◐ ✺ ✺ ◐ ✺ ◐ ✺ ◐ ✺

Reminder

- The **lowest common denominator** (LCD) is the smallest number both denominators will divide into evenly. This is called the **least common multiple** (LCM).
- The LCD is never smaller than the larger of the two denominators.
- Always try the larger denominator to see if both denominators will divide evenly into it.
- Multiply the larger denominator by 2 and see if both denominators will divide into it. If not, multiply by 3 or 4.
- If the denominators are prime numbers or next to each other in counting order, multiply them to find the LCD.

Examples: $\frac{3}{4}$ and $\frac{5}{6}$ $\frac{1}{4}$ and $\frac{1}{5}$
Multiply 6 x 2 = 12   Multiply 4 x 5 = 20
12 is the LCD   20 is the LCD

Directions: Find the LCD/LCM for each pair of fractions. The first two are done for you.

1. $\frac{2}{3}$ and $\frac{3}{4}$

    LCD = 12

2. $\frac{4}{8}$ and $\frac{1}{2}$

    LCD = 8

3. $\frac{5}{11}$ and $\frac{1}{3}$

    LCD =

4. $\frac{3}{12}$ and $\frac{1}{6}$

    LCD =

5. $\frac{1}{4}$ and $\frac{1}{5}$

    LCD =

6. $\frac{1}{2}$ and $\frac{1}{3}$

    LCD =

7. $\frac{5}{6}$ and $\frac{4}{8}$

    LCD =

8. $\frac{1}{3}$ and $\frac{2}{8}$

    LCD =

9. $\frac{6}{7}$ and $\frac{4}{8}$

    LCD =

10. $\frac{3}{7}$ and $\frac{1}{2}$

    LCD =

11. $\frac{4}{5}$ and $\frac{2}{6}$

    LCD =

12. $\frac{3}{12}$ and $\frac{2}{8}$

    LCD =

13. $\frac{9}{10}$ and $\frac{2}{4}$

    LCD =

14. $\frac{5}{12}$ and $\frac{2}{10}$

    LCD =

15. $\frac{3}{9}$ and $\frac{2}{3}$

    LCD =

16. $\frac{2}{9}$ and $\frac{2}{6}$

    LCD =

17. $\frac{3}{8}$ and $\frac{4}{10}$

    LCD =

18. $\frac{3}{14}$ and $\frac{2}{7}$

    LCD =

Practice 18

Reminder

To add or subtract fractions with unlike denominators, follow these steps:

1. Line up the fractions in the "ladder" form (stacked on top of each other).
2. Determine the lowest common denominator by finding the least common multiple of the two denominators.
3. Determine the new numerators using the "backward Z" technique. (Divide the unlike denominator into the common denominator and multiply the answer times the original numerator.)
4. Add or subtract the new numerators.
5. Bring down the common denominator.

$$\frac{3}{4} = \frac{9}{12}$$
$$-\frac{1}{3} = \frac{4}{12}$$
$$\frac{5}{12}$$

Directions: Find the lowest common denominator. Then add or subtract each problem. Reduce all answers to lowest terms. The first two are done for you.

1. $\dfrac{3}{6} = \dfrac{6}{12}$

$-\dfrac{1}{4} = \dfrac{3}{12}$

$\dfrac{3}{12} = \dfrac{1}{4}$

2. $\dfrac{1}{8} = \dfrac{3}{24}$

$+\dfrac{2}{6} = \dfrac{8}{24}$

$\dfrac{11}{24}$

3. $\dfrac{2}{4}$

$+\dfrac{1}{3}$

4. $\dfrac{4}{10}$

$-\dfrac{1}{5}$

5. $\dfrac{8}{12}$

$-\dfrac{3}{8}$

6. $\dfrac{1}{2}$

$+\dfrac{1}{3}$

7. $\dfrac{5}{9}$

$-\dfrac{1}{6}$

8. $\dfrac{5}{6}$

$-\dfrac{1}{4}$

9. $\dfrac{2}{3}$

$+\dfrac{5}{12}$

10. $\dfrac{1}{3}$

$+\dfrac{4}{5}$

11. $\dfrac{4}{9}$

$-\dfrac{1}{3}$

12. $\dfrac{13}{20}$

$-\dfrac{2}{4}$

13. $\dfrac{1}{5}$

$+\dfrac{1}{2}$

14. $\dfrac{4}{12}$

$+\dfrac{1}{4}$

15. $\dfrac{10}{12}$

$+\dfrac{3}{8}$

Practice 19

Reminder

Decimals are a kind of fraction based on 10 and multiples of 10, such as 100 and 1,000.

$$\frac{10}{100} = \frac{1}{10} = 0.1 \qquad \frac{1}{100} = 0.01 \qquad \frac{42}{100} = 0.42$$

Directions: Identify the fractions and decimals illustrated below. Write your answers next to each shape. The first one is done for you.

1. $\frac{20}{100} = 0.2$

2.

3.

4.

5.

6.

7.

8.

9.

10.

11.

12.

13.

14.

15.

Directions: Shade in the amount on each graph indicated by the fraction and decimal.

16. $\frac{3}{10} = 0.3$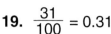

17. $\frac{6}{10} = 0.6$

18. $\frac{1}{10} = 0.1$

19. $\frac{31}{100} = 0.31$

20. $\frac{65}{100} = 0.65$

21. $\frac{92}{100} = 0.92$

Practice 20

Reminder

Decimals are a kind of fraction based on 10 and multiples of 10, such as 100 and 1,000.

$$\frac{25}{100} = 0.25 \qquad \frac{22}{100} = 0.22 \qquad \frac{3}{10} = 0.3 \qquad \frac{30}{100} = 0.30 \text{ or } 0.3$$

$$\frac{1}{10} = 0.1 = \frac{10}{100} = 0.10 \text{ (just as 1 dime equals 10 pennies)}$$
$$\frac{5}{10} = 0.5 = \frac{50}{100} = 0.50 \text{ (just as 5 dimes equals 50 pennies)}$$

0.5   =   0.50

Directions: Name the decimal for each fraction listed below. The first two are done for you.

1. $\frac{4}{10}$ = _____0.4_____

2. $\frac{61}{100}$ = _____0.61_____

3. $\frac{5}{10}$ = _____

4. $\frac{7}{10}$ = _____

5. $\frac{73}{100}$ = _____

6. $\frac{31}{100}$ = _____

7. $\frac{10}{10}$ = _____

8. $\frac{9}{10}$ = _____

9. $\frac{88}{100}$ = _____

10. $\frac{44}{100}$ = _____

11. $\frac{69}{100}$ = _____

12. $\frac{9}{100}$ = _____

13. $\frac{7}{100}$ = _____

14. $\frac{18}{100}$ = _____

15. $\frac{3}{100}$ = _____

Directions: Write these decimals as fractions in lowest terms. The first two are done for you.

16. 0.4 = _____$\frac{4}{10} = \frac{2}{5}$_____

17. 0.05 = _____$\frac{5}{100} = \frac{1}{20}$_____

18. 0.18 = _____

19. 0.13 = _____

20. 0.23 = _____

21. 0.47 = _____

22. 0.09 = _____

23. 0.01 = _____

24. 0.10 = _____

25. 0.57 = _____

26. 0.78 = _____

27. 0.20 = _____

28. 0.8 = _____

29. 0.08 = _____

30. 0.99 = _____

Practice 21

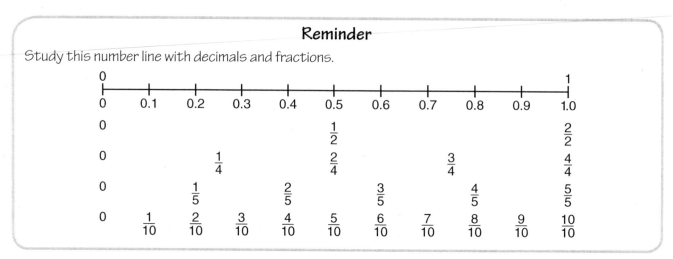

Directions: Use the number line to help you write the decimal equivalent for each fraction. The first two are done for you.

1. $\frac{3}{10}$ = _____ 0.3 _____

2. $\frac{1}{4}$ = _____ 0.25 _____

3. $\frac{1}{2}$ = _____

4. $\frac{7}{10}$ = _____

5. $\frac{4}{5}$ = _____

6. $\frac{9}{10}$ = _____

7. $\frac{10}{10}$ = _____

8. $\frac{6}{10}$ = _____

9. $\frac{3}{5}$ = _____

10. $\frac{1}{5}$ = _____

11. $\frac{2}{5}$ = _____

12. $\frac{3}{4}$ = _____

13. $\frac{5}{5}$ = _____

14. $\frac{2}{4}$ = _____

15. $\frac{8}{10}$ = _____

Directions: Use the number line to help you convert these decimals to fractions in lowest terms. The first two are done for you.

16. 0.25 = _____ $\frac{25}{100} = \frac{1}{4}$ _____

17. 0.4 = _____ $\frac{4}{10} = \frac{2}{5}$ _____

18. 0.6 = _____

19. 0.5 = _____

20. 0.7 = _____

21. 0.2 = _____

22. 0.3 = _____

23. 0.9 = _____

24. 0.1 = _____

25. 0.75 = _____

26. 0.8 = _____

27. 1.0 = _____

28. Which decimal on a number line would equal 20¢? _____

29. Which decimal on a number line would equal 50¢? _____

30. Which fraction on a number line would equal 25¢? _____

Practice 22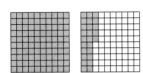

Reminder

These illustrations show decimals greater than 1.

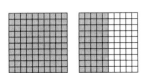 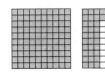 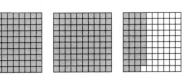

Decimal values: 1.25   1.48   2.78

Mixed numbers: $1\frac{25}{100} = 1\frac{1}{4}$ $1\frac{48}{100} = 1\frac{12}{25}$ $2\frac{78}{100} = 2\frac{39}{50}$

Directions: Write the decimal and mixed number for each graph. The first one is done for you.

1.
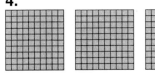

decimal = 1.5

mixed number = $1\frac{50}{100} = 1\frac{1}{2}$

2.
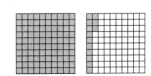

decimal = _____

mixed number = _____

3.
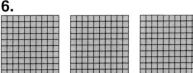

decimal = _____

mixed number = _____

4.

decimal = _____

mixed number = _____

5.

decimal = _____

mixed number = _____

6.

decimal = _____

mixed number = _____

Directions: Convert these mixed numbers to decimals. The first one is done for you.

7. $1\frac{3}{4} = $ ____1.75____

8. $1\frac{6}{10} = $ _____

9. $1\frac{2}{10} = $ _____

10. $2\frac{5}{10} = $ _____

11. $4\frac{3}{10} = $ _____

12. $5\frac{41}{100} = $ _____

13. $7\frac{1}{10} = $ _____

14. $2\frac{6}{100} = $ _____

15. $1\frac{31}{100} = $ _____

16. $1\frac{7}{100} = $ _____

17. $5\frac{91}{100} = $ _____

18. $3\frac{9}{100} = $ _____

19. $4\frac{22}{100} = $ _____

20. $1\frac{3}{100} = $ _____

21. $2\frac{1}{4} = $ _____

Practice 23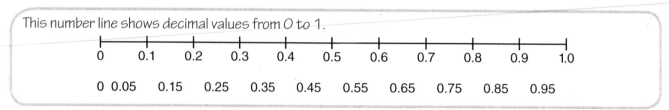

This number line shows decimal values from 0 to 1.

```
  +----+----+----+----+----+----+----+----+----+----+
  0   0.1  0.2  0.3  0.4  0.5  0.6  0.7  0.8  0.9  1.0
```

  0 0.05   0.15   0.25   0.35   0.45   0.55   0.65   0.75   0.85   0.95

Directions: Use the number line to help you compare decimals values. Write > (greater than), < (less than), or = (equal to) in the spaces below. The first two are done for you.

1. 0.35 ____<____ 0.5   **2.** 1.0 ____>____ 0.9   **3.** 0.4 _____ 0.7

4. 0.6 _____ 0.75   **5.** 1.0 _____ 0.1   **6.** 0.95 _____ 0.8

7. 0.05 _____ 0.5   **8.** 0.6 _____ 0.60   **9.** 0.85 _____ 0.9

10. 0.7 _____ 0.60   **11.** 0.45 _____ 0.4   **12.** 0.7 _____ 0.85

13. 1.0 _____ 0.85   **14.** 0.95 _____ 0.9   **15.** 0.70 _____ 0.7

This number line shows decimal values from 0 to 5.

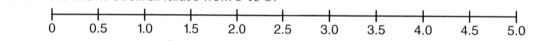

```
  +----+----+----+----+----+----+----+----+----+----+
  0   0.5  1.0  1.5  2.0  2.5  3.0  3.5  4.0  4.5  5.0
```

Directions: Use the number line to help you compare decimals values. Write > (greater than), < (less than), or = (equal to) in the spaces below. The first one is done for you.

16. 2.5 ____<____ 3.0   **17.** 4.5 _____ 4.0   **18.** 4.0 _____ 1.5

19. 0.5 _____ 5.0   **20.** 1.0 _____ 0.5   **21.** 3 _____ 3.0

22. 5 _____ 4.5   **23.** 3.5 _____ 5   **24.** 2.5 _____ 2.0

25. 2.1 _____ 1.2   **26.** 3.75 _____ 3.8   **27.** 3.58 _____ 4.1

28. 4.7 _____ 3.95   **29.** 4.75 _____ 4.8   **30.** 3.0 _____ 1.75

31. 2.50 _____ 2.5   **32.** 4.5 _____ 3.95   **33.** 2.98 _____ 3.0

Practice 24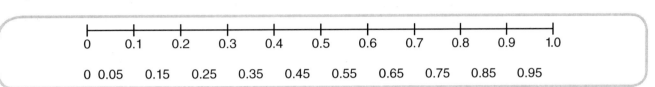

```
  |----|----|----|----|----|----|----|----|----|----|
  0   0.1  0.2  0.3  0.4  0.5  0.6  0.7  0.8  0.9  1.0

    0  0.05  0.15  0.25  0.35  0.45  0.55  0.65  0.75  0.85  0.95
```

Directions: Use the number line to place these decimals in order from **least to greatest**. The first two are done for you.

1. 0.05   _0.05_
     0.5   _0.25_
     0.25   _0.5_

2. 0.75   _0.50_
     0.50   _0.75_
     0.85   _0.85_

3. 0.65 _____
     0.20 _____
     0.40 _____

4. 0.81 _____
     0.8 _____
     0.08 _____

5. 0.63 _____
     0.6 _____
     0.53 _____

6. 0.04 _____
     0.40 _____
     0.44 _____

7. 0.96 _____
     0.69 _____
     0.09 _____

8. 0.35 _____
     0.53 _____
     0.05 _____

9. 0.89 _____
     0.9 _____
     0.91 _____

10. 0.21 _____
     0.12 _____
     0.2 _____

11. 0.46 _____
     0.5 _____
     0.04 _____

12. 0.9 _____
     0.09 _____
     0.89 _____

```
  |----|----|----|----|----|----|----|----|----|----|
  0   0.5  1.0  1.5  2.0  2.5  3.0  3.5  4.0  4.5  5.0
```

Directions: Use the two number lines to help you place these decimals in order from **least to greatest**. The first two are done for you.

13. 2.1   _0.12_
     0.12   _0.21_
     0.21   _2.1_

14. 3.63   _0.04_
     4.6   _3.63_
     0.04   _4.6_

15. 5.6 _____
     0.65 _____
     0.06 _____

16. 0.34 _____
     0.3 _____
     3.03 _____

17. 0.08 _____
     0.8 _____
     8.0 _____

18. 0.05 _____
     5.01 _____
     3.05 _____

19. 5.81 _____
     5.18 _____
     0.5 _____

20. 3.18 _____
     0.31 _____
     0.3 _____

21. 0.1 _____
     0.01 _____
     1.0 _____

22. 2.4 _____
     2.42 _____
     4.02 _____

23. 5.05 _____
     0.55 _____
     5.5 _____

24. 2.14 _____
     1.24 _____
     2.41 _____

Practice 25

Reminder

In the numeral **43.26**

  4 = **tens** place
  3 = **ones** place
  2 = **tenths** place
  6 = **hundredths** place

When rounding to a specific place value, look at the digit one place to its right.

- If the digit is 5 or greater, round up.
- If the digit is less than 5, round down.

To round 43.26 to the nearest whole number, find the ones place (3). Now look one digit to its right (2). 2 is less than 5, so 43.26 rounds down to 43.

To round 43.26 to the nearest tenth, find the tenths place (2). Now look one digit to its right (6). 6 is greater than 5, so 43.26 rounds up to 43.3.

Directions: Round these decimals to the nearest **whole number**. The first two are done for you.

1. 5.36 _____5_____   **2.** 7.8 _____8_____   **3.** 0.56 _____

4. 7.96 _____   **5.** 8.19 _____   **6.** 4.5 _____

7. 8.51 _____   **8.** 2.99 _____   **9.** 3.55 _____

10. 6.77 _____   **11.** 3.49 _____   **12.** 3.50 _____

13. 2.1 _____   **14.** 2.05 _____   **15.** 6.73 _____

Directions: Round these decimals to the nearest **tenth**. The first two are done for you.

16. 0.46 _____0.5_____   **17.** 2.35 _____2.4_____   **18.** 0.83 _____

19. 3.94 _____   **20.** 2.99 _____   **21.** 0.89 _____

22. 1.76 _____   **23.** 0.23 _____   **24.** 0.55 _____

25. 0.61 _____   **26.** 3.85 _____   **27.** 0.37 _____

28. 0.05 _____   **29.** 5.60 _____   **30.** 4.45 _____

31. 2.49 _____   **32.** 9.99 _____   **33.** 6.06 _____

34. 79.75 _____   **35.** 27.84 _____   **36.** 0.99 _____

Practice 26 ❧ ❧ ❧ ❧ ❧ ❧ ❧ ❧ ❧ ❧

Reminder

To add decimals:

1. Use the ladder form.
2. Line up the decimals.
3. Use placeholder zeroes (if needed).
4. Add the numbers (carry where necessary).
5. Line up the decimal in your answer with the decimals from the problem.

$3.2 + 0.61 =$

3.20 ← (placeholder zero)
$+ 0.61$
3.81 ← (decimal stays two places to the left)

Directions: Use the reminder above to correctly add these decimals. The first two are done for you.

1. 3.52 + 5.90 9.42	**2.** 5.60 + 0.66 6.26	**3.** 0.23 + 9.1	**4.** 0.41 + 5.5
5. 8.01 + 0.99	**6.** 4.5 + 16.51	**7.** 0.3 + 7.46	**8.** 1.98 + 0.9
9. 6.71 + 45.3	**10.** 9.99 + 0.01	**11.** 6.6 + 6.66	**12.** 4.1 + 35.99

13. 23.1 + 6.6 =

14. 6.99 + 0.02 =

15. 56.07 + 2.09 =

16. 0.5 + 0.87 =

17. 9.09 + 33.92 =

18. 4.1 + 0.01 =

19. 6.07 + 66.7 =

20. 99.1 + 9.91 =

21. 1.1 + 0.11 =

22. 22.12 + 0.2 =

23. 9.9 + 0.99 =

24. 6.06 + 0.6 =

25. 6 + 3.3 =

26. 7.3 + 9 =

27. 20 + 0.01 =

Practice 27 ✺ ๑ ✺ ✺ ๑ ✺ ๑ ✺ ๑ ✺

Reminder

To subtract decimals:

1. Use the ladder form.
2. Line up the decimals.
3. Use placeholder zeroes (if needed).
4. Subtract the numbers (borrow/regroup where necessary).
5. Line up the decimal in your answer with the decimals from the problem.

$5.1 - 3.25 =$

5.10 ← (placeholder zero)
$- 3.25$

1.85 ← (decimal stays two places to the left)

Directions: Use the reminder above to correctly subtract these decimals. The first two are done for you.

1. $\begin{array}{r} 7.20 \\ -\ 2.34 \\ \hline 4.86 \end{array}$

2. $\begin{array}{r} 0.50 \\ -\ 0.47 \\ \hline 0.03 \end{array}$

3. $\begin{array}{r} 8.6 \\ -\ 7.99 \\ \hline \end{array}$

4. $\begin{array}{r} 67.6 \\ -\ 8.77 \\ \hline \end{array}$

5. $\begin{array}{r} 7.01 \\ -\ 2.94 \\ \hline \end{array}$

6. $\begin{array}{r} 9.1 \\ -\ 5.32 \\ \hline \end{array}$

7. $\begin{array}{r} 0.9 \\ -\ 0.89 \\ \hline \end{array}$

8. $\begin{array}{r} 29.1 \\ -\ 10.99 \\ \hline \end{array}$

9. $\begin{array}{r} 6.71 \\ -\ 5.52 \\ \hline \end{array}$

10. $\begin{array}{r} 73.02 \\ -\ 59.13 \\ \hline \end{array}$

11. $\begin{array}{r} 9.01 \\ -\ 6.92 \\ \hline \end{array}$

12. $\begin{array}{r} 7.1 \\ -\ 6.99 \\ \hline \end{array}$

13. $6.1 - 3.9 =$

14. $7 - 3.9 =$

15. $13.1 - 12.09 =$

16. $1.0 - 0.01 =$

17. $13 - 12.99 =$

18. $12.01 - 11.98 =$

19. $1.19 - 0.17 =$

20. $15 - 14.2 =$

21. $9.0 - 6.77 =$

22. $8 - 6.02 =$

23. $77.2 - 77.02 =$

24. $101 - 1.01 =$

25. $1 - 0.78 =$

26. $2.1 - 1.21 =$

27. $33 - 3.03 =$

Practice 28

Directions: Round each decimal to the nearest whole number, then estimate the sums or differences. The first two are done for you.

1.
$$\begin{array}{r} 3.56 \\ -\ 1.7 \\ \hline \end{array} \quad \begin{array}{r} 4 \\ -\ 2 \\ \hline 2 \end{array}$$

2.
$$\begin{array}{r} 7.5 \\ +\ 3.39 \\ \hline \end{array} \quad \begin{array}{r} 8 \\ +\ 3 \\ \hline 11 \end{array}$$

3.
$$\begin{array}{r} 2.1 \\ -\ 1.99 \\ \hline \end{array}$$

4.
$$\begin{array}{r} 9.3 \\ +\ 5.6 \\ \hline \end{array}$$

5.
$$\begin{array}{r} 8.09 \\ -\ 4.99 \\ \hline \end{array}$$

6.
$$\begin{array}{r} 7.5 \\ +\ 8.49 \\ \hline \end{array}$$

7.
$$\begin{array}{r} 8.09 \\ -\ 4.1 \\ \hline \end{array}$$

8.
$$\begin{array}{r} 6.5 \\ +\ 9.4 \\ \hline \end{array}$$

9.
$$\begin{array}{r} 9.19 \\ -\ 8.5 \\ \hline \end{array}$$

10.
$$\begin{array}{r} 3.01 \\ -\ 2.9 \\ \hline \end{array}$$

11.
$$\begin{array}{r} 6.06 \\ +\ 5.5 \\ \hline \end{array}$$

12.
$$\begin{array}{r} 14.44 \\ +\ 6 \\ \hline \end{array}$$

13. $67.0 - 6.99 =$

14. $17 - 7.99 =$

15. $23.1 + 2.31 =$

16. $9 - 3.5 =$

17. $28.1 - 27.99 =$

18. $4.01 + 40.1 =$

19. $6.6 + 66.6 =$

20. $40.01 - 20.9 =$

21. $23 + 3.02 =$

22. $9.09 - 8.9 =$

23. $100 - 1.01 =$

24. $99 - 98.5 =$

Practice 29

Directions: Use your skills in adding and subtracting decimals to complete these operations with money. The first two are done for you.

1. $3.47
    + $2.58
    $6.05

2. $4.00
    − $2.17
    $1.83

3. $7.05
    + $6.97

4. $13.00
    − $9.23

5. $8.88
    + $3.71

6. $11.01
    − $7.12

7. $8.04
    − $5.13

8. $16.66
    + $13.34

9. $7.07
    − $1.18

10. $34.14
    − $12.45

11. $40.00
    − $11.25

12. $33.03
    + $98.98

13. $22.69
    + $54.59

14. $60.01
    − $15.99

15. $0.31
    + $9.99

16. $4.00 − $3.89 =

17. $76.21 + $23.13 =

18. $424.44 + $399.99 =

19. $111.00 − $89.97 =

20. $100.00 − $16.66 =

21. $1.38 + $0.72 =

22. $50.00 − $49.95 =

23. $33.33 + $67.67 =

24. $13.78 + $77.23 =

25. $99.99 + $88.88 =

26. $200.00 − $123.89 =

27. $3.03 − $0.69 =

Practice 30

Reminder

- Percent means "of 100."
- All percents are fractional parts of 100.
- This sign means percent: %

The shaded part of the first graph shows 25% because 25 of the 100 squares are shaded. This means that 75% are not shaded.

The shaded part of the second graph shows 42% because 42 of the 100 squares are shaded. This means that 58% is not shaded.

Directions: Write the percent shaded next to each graph.

1.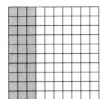

2.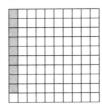

3.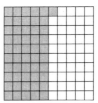

4.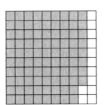

5.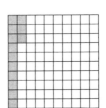

6.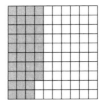

7.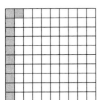

8.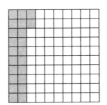

9.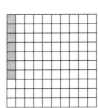

10.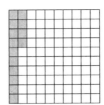

11.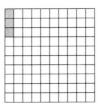

12.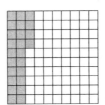

13.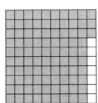

14.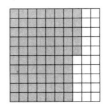

15.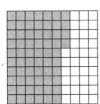

Practice 31

Directions: Shade in the percent listed above each graph. The first one is done for you.

1. 32%

2. 45%

3. 78%

4. 99%

5. 12%

6. 4%

7. 50%

8. 29%

9. 66%
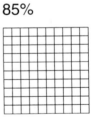

10. 19%

11. 6%

12. 85%
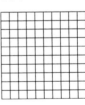

13. 40%

14. 80%

15. 33%

16. 2%

17. 92%
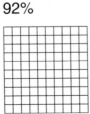

18. 100%

Practice 32 ❡ ❡ ❡ ❡ ❡ ❡ ❡ ❡ ❡ ❡ ❡

> ### Reminder
> - Percent means "of 100."
> - All percents are fractional parts of 100.
> - Decimals expressed in hundredths are equal to percents.
>   Examples: 0.15 = 15%   0.48 = 48%
> - Decimals expressed in tenths can be converted to hundredths and then to percents.
>   Examples: 0.1 = 0.10 = 10%   0.3 = 0.30 = 30%

Directions: Convert these decimals to percents. The first one is done for you.

1. 0.2 = _____20%_____

2. 0.19 = _____

3. 0.34 = _____

4. 0.57 = _____

5. 0.5 = _____

6. 0.01 = _____

7. 0.03 = _____

8. 0.8 = _____

9. 0.11 = _____

10. 0.14 = _____

11. 0.99 = _____

12. 0.67 = _____

13. 0.78 = _____

14. 0.86 = _____

15. 0.61 = _____

16. 0.13 = _____

17. 0.3 = _____

18. 0.50 = _____

19. 0.1 = _____

20. 0.77 = _____

21. 0.07 = _____

22. 0.06 = _____

23. 0.41 = _____

24. 0.04 = _____

25. 0.75 = _____

26. 0.09 = _____

27. 0.9 = _____

28. 0.02 = _____

29. 0.6 = _____

30. 0.0 = _____

31. 0.37 = _____

32. 0.88 = _____

33. 0.26 = _____

34. 0.18 = _____

35. 0.23 = _____

36. 0.47 = _____

Practice 33

Reminder

- All percents are fractional parts of 100.
- Decimals expressed in hundredths are equal to percents.
  Examples: $0.25 = 25\%$ $0.44 = 44\%$
- Percents ending in zero are equal to decimals expressed in tenths.
  Examples: $20\% = 0.20 = 0.2$ $90\% = 0.90 = 0.9$
- Percents over 100 can be expressed by a whole number and a decimal.
  Examples: $128\% = 1.28$ $234\% = 2.34$

Directions: Convert these percents to decimals expressed in hundredths or tenths. The first two are done for you.

1. $40\% =$ _____0.4_____

2. $3\% =$ _____0.03_____

3. $33\% =$ _____

4. $50\% =$ _____

5. $66\% =$ _____

6. $99\% =$ _____

7. $91\% =$ _____

8. $54\% =$ _____

9. $80\% =$ _____

10. $61\% =$ _____

11. $12\% =$ _____

12. $4\% =$ _____

13. $21\% =$ _____

14. $9\% =$ _____

15. $18\% =$ _____

16. $2\% =$ _____

17. $69\% =$ _____

18. $19\% =$ _____

19. $231\% =$ _____

20. $156\% =$ _____

21. $101\% =$ _____

22. $111\% =$ _____

23. $299\% =$ _____

24. $209\% =$ _____

25. $140\% =$ _____

26. $155\% =$ _____

27. $110\% =$ _____

28. $300\% =$ _____

29. $30\% =$ _____

30. $3\% =$ _____

31. $60\% =$ _____

32. $6\% =$ _____

33. $106\% =$ _____

Practice 34 ☙ ঙ ❧ ❧ ঙ ❧ ঙ ❧ ঙ ❧

Directions: Convert these percents to fractions expressed in hundredths or tenths. Reduce the fractions to lowest terms. The first two are done for you.

1. $50\% = \underline{\dfrac{50}{100} = \dfrac{1}{2}}$

2. $25\% = \underline{\dfrac{25}{100} = \dfrac{1}{4}}$

3. $19\% = \underline{\hspace{3cm}}$

4. $6\% = \underline{\hspace{3cm}}$

5. $90\% = \underline{\hspace{3cm}}$

6. $40\% = \underline{\hspace{3cm}}$

7. $22\% = \underline{\hspace{3cm}}$

8. $16\% = \underline{\hspace{3cm}}$

9. $31\% = \underline{\hspace{3cm}}$

10. $70\% = \underline{\hspace{3cm}}$

11. $66\% = \underline{\hspace{3cm}}$

12. $37\% = \underline{\hspace{3cm}}$

13. $91\% = \underline{\hspace{3cm}}$

14. $12\% = \underline{\hspace{3cm}}$

15. $3\% = \underline{\hspace{3cm}}$

Directions: Convert these fractions to percents. You may have to divide the denominator into 100 and multiply that answer by the numerator. The first two are done for you.

16. $\dfrac{1}{4} = \underline{\dfrac{25}{100} = 25\%}$

17. $\dfrac{1}{5} = \underline{\dfrac{20}{100} = 20\%}$

18. $\dfrac{3}{10} = \underline{\hspace{2.5cm}}$

19. $\dfrac{1}{2} = \underline{\hspace{2.5cm}}$

20. $\dfrac{7}{10} = \underline{\hspace{2.5cm}}$

21. $\dfrac{5}{10} = \underline{\hspace{2.5cm}}$

22. $\dfrac{9}{10} = \underline{\hspace{2.5cm}}$

23. $\dfrac{71}{100} = \underline{\hspace{2.5cm}}$

24. $\dfrac{38}{100} = \underline{\hspace{2.5cm}}$

25. $\dfrac{2}{5} = \underline{\hspace{2.5cm}}$

26. $\dfrac{3}{4} = \underline{\hspace{2.5cm}}$

27. $\dfrac{8}{10} = \underline{\hspace{2.5cm}}$

28. $\dfrac{33}{100} = \underline{\hspace{2.5cm}}$

29. $\dfrac{6}{10} = \underline{\hspace{2.5cm}}$

30. $\dfrac{27}{100} = \underline{\hspace{2.5cm}}$

31. $\dfrac{4}{100} = \underline{\hspace{2.5cm}}$

32. $\dfrac{3}{100} = \underline{\hspace{2.5cm}}$

33. $\dfrac{4}{5} = \underline{\hspace{2.5cm}}$

Practice 35 🐚 🐚 🐚 🐚 🐚 🐚 🐚 🐚 🐚 🐚

Reminder

The figure below illustrates 225%.

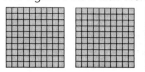

$$225\% = 2.25 = 2\frac{1}{4}$$

Directions: Write the equivalent percents for these decimals and fractions over 100. The first two are done for you.

1. 2.5 = _____250%_____

2. $1\frac{3}{4}$ = _____175%_____

3. 2.17 = _____

4. 5.51 = _____

5. $1\frac{1}{2}$ = _____

6. 3.19 = _____

7. 1.99 = _____

8. $4\frac{1}{2}$ = _____

9. $3\frac{1}{2}$ = _____

10. $2\frac{1}{5}$ = _____

11. 7.01 = _____

12. 3.03 = _____

13. 4.0 = _____

14. $6\frac{1}{4}$ = _____

15. $5\frac{1}{5}$ = _____

16. $1\frac{4}{5}$ = _____

17. 1.8 = _____

18. 1.08 = _____

19. 3.21 = _____

20. $5\frac{3}{6}$ = _____

21. $3\frac{1}{4}$ = _____

22. 5.98 = _____

23. 6.01 = _____

24. 8.24 = _____

25. 1.33 = _____

26. 3.33 = _____

27. $2\frac{1}{10}$ = _____

28. $3\frac{3}{10}$ = _____

29. 5.23 = _____

30. $2\frac{7}{10}$ = _____

31. $1\frac{1}{5}$ = _____

32. 4.16 = _____

33. 1.79 = _____

Practice 36 ☙ ∂ ☙ ☙ ∂ ☙ ∂ ☙ ∂ ☙

Reminder

Percents are computed this way: 25% of 60 =

1. Convert the percent to a decimal: 25% = 0.25
2. Multiply the decimal times the whole number using the ladder form.
3. Keep the decimal in the answer the same number of places to the left as there are decimal places in the original multiplication problem. In this case, it is two places to the left.

```
       60
   x 0.25
      300
   +1200
   15.00   Answer = 15
```

Directions: Compute the percents of each number listed below. The first two are done for you.

1. 30% of 50 = 15
```
      50
 x  0.30
   15.00
```

2. 24% of 40 = 9.6
```
      40
 x  0.24
     160
 +   800
    9.60
```

3. 50% of 68 =
```
      68
 x  0.50
```

4. 20% of 58 =

5. 9% of 90 =

6. 70% of 50 =

7. 40% of 200 =

8. 60% of 40 =

9. 25% of 80 =

10. 15% of 48 =

11. 60% of 20 =

12. 75% of 80 =

13. 11% of 44 =

14. 25% of 60 =

15. 3% of 200 =

16. 44% of 80 =

17. 36% of 60 =

18. 22% of 50 =

Test Practice 1

Directions: Identify the equivalent fraction for each fraction listed.

1. $\frac{1}{3}$ =

    Ⓐ $\frac{2}{4}$ Ⓑ $\frac{3}{6}$ Ⓒ $\frac{3}{9}$ Ⓓ $\frac{8}{12}$

2. $\frac{9}{12}$ =

    Ⓐ $\frac{1}{2}$ Ⓑ $\frac{3}{4}$ Ⓒ $\frac{6}{9}$ Ⓓ $\frac{3}{5}$

3. $\frac{4}{5}$ =

    Ⓐ $\frac{7}{10}$ Ⓑ $\frac{3}{4}$ Ⓒ $\frac{16}{20}$ Ⓓ $\frac{7}{8}$

4. $\frac{1}{4}$ =

    Ⓐ $\frac{2}{8}$ Ⓑ $\frac{2}{5}$ Ⓒ $\frac{2}{6}$ Ⓓ $\frac{3}{10}$

5. $\frac{3}{3}$ =

    Ⓐ $\frac{11}{4}$ Ⓑ $\frac{4}{5}$ Ⓒ 1   Ⓓ $\frac{7}{8}$

6. $\frac{6}{2}$ =

    Ⓐ 3   Ⓑ 4   Ⓒ $\frac{9}{4}$ Ⓓ $\frac{8}{4}$

7. $\frac{3}{5}$ =

    Ⓐ $\frac{6}{10}$ Ⓑ $\frac{7}{10}$ Ⓒ $\frac{7}{3}$ Ⓓ $\frac{9}{10}$

8. $\frac{10}{8}$ =

    Ⓐ $\frac{5}{4}$ Ⓑ $\frac{5}{6}$ Ⓒ $\frac{4}{3}$ Ⓓ $\frac{11}{3}$

Directions: Determine which letter represents a fraction greater than (>) the fraction listed for each number.

9. $\frac{7}{12}$

    Ⓐ $\frac{5}{6}$ Ⓑ $\frac{1}{3}$ Ⓒ $\frac{1}{2}$ Ⓓ $\frac{4}{9}$

10. $\frac{5}{6}$

    Ⓐ $\frac{3}{5}$ Ⓑ $\frac{11}{12}$ Ⓒ $\frac{2}{3}$ Ⓓ $\frac{3}{4}$

11. $\frac{1}{2}$

    Ⓐ $\frac{1}{3}$ Ⓑ $\frac{1}{4}$ Ⓒ $\frac{2}{6}$ Ⓓ $\frac{3}{5}$

12. $\frac{1}{3}$

    Ⓐ $\frac{2}{6}$ Ⓑ $\frac{1}{2}$ Ⓒ $\frac{1}{4}$ Ⓓ $\frac{2}{8}$

13. $\frac{3}{4}$

    Ⓐ $\frac{6}{8}$ Ⓑ $\frac{3}{5}$ Ⓒ $\frac{9}{12}$ Ⓓ $\frac{5}{6}$

14. $\frac{2}{3}$

    Ⓐ $\frac{5}{6}$ Ⓑ $\frac{2}{4}$ Ⓒ $\frac{4}{6}$ Ⓓ $\frac{7}{12}$

Directions: Determine the fraction that is not equivalent to the given fraction.

15. $\frac{1}{2}$

    Ⓐ $\frac{2}{4}$ Ⓑ $\frac{3}{6}$ Ⓒ $\frac{4}{7}$ Ⓓ $\frac{5}{10}$

16. $\frac{1}{3}$

    Ⓐ $\frac{2}{6}$ Ⓑ $\frac{3}{9}$ Ⓒ $\frac{4}{8}$ Ⓓ $\frac{6}{18}$

17. $\frac{1}{4}$

    Ⓐ $\frac{2}{8}$ Ⓑ $\frac{3}{10}$ Ⓒ $\frac{3}{12}$ Ⓓ $\frac{4}{16}$

18. $\frac{2}{3}$

    Ⓐ $\frac{6}{9}$ Ⓑ $\frac{8}{10}$ Ⓒ $\frac{10}{15}$ Ⓓ $\frac{8}{12}$

19. $\frac{5}{10}$

    Ⓐ $\frac{1}{2}$ Ⓑ $\frac{2}{4}$ Ⓒ $\frac{2}{3}$ Ⓓ $\frac{3}{6}$

20. $\frac{3}{4}$

    Ⓐ $\frac{9}{12}$ Ⓑ $\frac{4}{8}$ Ⓒ $\frac{6}{8}$ Ⓓ $\frac{15}{20}$

Test Practice 2

Directions: Identify the fraction in each set that is in lowest terms.

1. (A) $\frac{3}{6}$ (B) $\frac{4}{8}$ (C) $\frac{4}{7}$ (D) $\frac{5}{15}$ 2. (A) $\frac{1}{2}$ (B) $\frac{4}{10}$ (C) $\frac{3}{12}$ (D) $\frac{7}{21}$

3. (A) $\frac{4}{14}$ (B) $\frac{3}{9}$ (C) $\frac{3}{3}$ (D) $\frac{5}{8}$ 4. (A) $\frac{8}{8}$ (B) $\frac{6}{10}$ (C) $\frac{2}{3}$ (D) $\frac{12}{18}$

5. (A) $\frac{3}{5}$ (B) $\frac{4}{6}$ (C) $\frac{3}{12}$ (D) $\frac{2}{8}$ 6. (A) $\frac{6}{6}$ (B) $\frac{8}{6}$ (C) $\frac{4}{8}$ (D) $\frac{7}{8}$

Directions: Compute the sums or differences. Reduce to lowest terms.

7. $\frac{3}{4} - \frac{2}{4} =$

   (A) $\frac{4}{8}$ (B) $\frac{5}{16}$ (C) $\frac{1}{4}$ (D) $\frac{4}{8}$

8. $\frac{3}{8} + \frac{2}{8} =$

   (A) $\frac{5}{4}$ (B) $\frac{1}{8}$ (C) $\frac{1}{16}$ (D) $\frac{5}{8}$

9. $\frac{7}{8} - \frac{4}{8} =$

   (A) $\frac{3}{16}$ (B) $\frac{3}{8}$ (C) $\frac{1}{4}$ (D) $\frac{11}{8}$

10. $\frac{7}{12} + \frac{4}{12} =$

    (A) $\frac{12}{12}$ (B) $\frac{11}{24}$ (C) $\frac{3}{12}$ (D) $\frac{11}{12}$

11. $\frac{9}{12} - \frac{5}{12} =$

    (A) $\frac{4}{24}$ (B) $\frac{1}{3}$ (C) $\frac{14}{12}$ (D) $\frac{1}{2}$

12. $\frac{5}{7} + \frac{2}{7} =$

    (A) $\frac{3}{7}$ (B) $\frac{4}{7}$ (C) 1 (D) $\frac{7}{14}$

Directions: Convert these improper fractions to the correct value in mixed numbers or whole numbers.

13. $\frac{8}{3} =$

    (A) $2\frac{1}{2}$ (B) $2\frac{2}{3}$ (C) $2\frac{1}{3}$ (D) 3

14. $\frac{4}{2} =$

    (A) $2\frac{1}{2}$ (B) 3 (C) $1\frac{1}{2}$ (D) 2

15. $\frac{6}{2} =$

    (A) 3 (B) $2\frac{2}{3}$ (C) $2\frac{1}{2}$ (D) $1\frac{1}{6}$

16. $\frac{7}{4} =$

    (A) $1\frac{4}{3}$ (B) $1\frac{4}{7}$ (C) $2\frac{1}{7}$ (D) $1\frac{3}{4}$

17. $\frac{11}{3} =$

    (A) $4\frac{1}{3}$ (B) $3\frac{1}{3}$ (C) $1\frac{1}{3}$ (D) $3\frac{2}{3}$

18. $\frac{21}{5} =$

    (A) $2\frac{1}{5}$ (B) $4\frac{1}{5}$ (C) $5\frac{1}{2}$ (D) $5\frac{1}{4}$

19. $\frac{3}{1} =$

    (A) $\frac{1}{3}$ (B) 3 (C) 4 (D) $2\frac{1}{3}$

20. $\frac{11}{10} =$

    (A) $1\frac{3}{10}$ (B) $1\frac{1}{2}$ (C) $1\frac{1}{11}$ (D) $1\frac{1}{10}$

Test Practice 3

Directions: Determine the lowest common denominator for each pair of fractions.

1. $\frac{3}{4}$ and $\frac{5}{6}$

   (A) 24   (B) 8   (C) 12   (D) 10

2. $\frac{1}{9}$ and $\frac{3}{6}$

   (A) 6   (B) 24   (C) 15   (D) 18

3. $\frac{1}{9}$ and $\frac{3}{4}$

   (A) 9   (B) 36   (C) 18   (D) 27

4. $\frac{1}{8}$ and $\frac{2}{3}$

   (A) 12   (B) 24   (C) 8   (D) 15

5. $\frac{1}{4}$ and $\frac{3}{10}$

   (A) 10   (B) 20   (C) 40   (D) 12

6. $\frac{3}{4}$ and $\frac{2}{5}$

   (A) 9   (B) 10   (C) 12   (D) 20

Directions: Put these fractions in order from least to greatest.

7. $\frac{2}{3}, \frac{3}{4}, \frac{1}{2}$

   (A) $\frac{1}{2}, \frac{3}{4}, \frac{2}{3}$ (B) $\frac{2}{3}, \frac{1}{2}, \frac{3}{4}$

   (C) $\frac{1}{2}, \frac{2}{3}, \frac{3}{4}$ (D) $\frac{3}{4}, \frac{1}{2}, \frac{2}{3}$

8. $\frac{1}{2}, \frac{1}{3}, \frac{1}{4}$

   (A) $\frac{1}{3}, \frac{1}{2}, \frac{1}{4}$ (B) $\frac{1}{2}, \frac{1}{3}, \frac{1}{4}$

   (C) $\frac{1}{2}, \frac{1}{4}, \frac{1}{3}$ (D) $\frac{1}{4}, \frac{1}{3}, \frac{1}{2}$

9. $\frac{3}{6}, \frac{3}{4}, \frac{2}{5}$

   (A) $\frac{1}{2}, \frac{1}{4}, \frac{3}{8}$ (B) $\frac{3}{6}, \frac{2}{5}, \frac{3}{4}$

   (C) $\frac{2}{5}, \frac{3}{4}, \frac{3}{6}$ (D) $\frac{2}{5}, \frac{3}{6}, \frac{3}{4}$

10. $\frac{3}{8}, \frac{1}{2}, \frac{1}{4}$

    (A) $\frac{3}{4}, \frac{3}{6}, \frac{2}{5}$ (B) $\frac{1}{4}, \frac{3}{8}, \frac{1}{2}$

    (C) $\frac{1}{2}, \frac{3}{8}, \frac{1}{4}$ (D) $\frac{1}{4}, \frac{1}{2}, \frac{3}{8}$

Directions: Add or subtract these fractions using the lowest common denominator.

11. $\frac{1}{2} + \frac{1}{3} =$

    (A) $\frac{4}{6}$ (B) $\frac{5}{5}$ (C) $\frac{5}{6}$ (D) $\frac{2}{5}$

12. $\frac{3}{4} - \frac{1}{6} =$

    (A) $\frac{7}{12}$ (B) $\frac{3}{4}$ (C) $\frac{2}{10}$ (D) $\frac{2}{6}$

13. $\frac{2}{5} + \frac{1}{2} =$

    (A) $\frac{3}{7}$ (B) $\frac{3}{10}$ (C) $\frac{8}{10}$ (D) $\frac{9}{10}$

14. $\frac{5}{6} - \frac{1}{4} =$

    (A) $\frac{4}{6}$ (B) $\frac{13}{12}$ (C) $\frac{6}{12}$ (D) $\frac{7}{12}$

15. $\frac{3}{4} - \frac{2}{3} =$

    (A) $\frac{1}{12}$ (B) $\frac{13}{12}$ (C) $\frac{1}{4}$ (D) $\frac{1}{3}$

16. $\frac{7}{9} - \frac{3}{6} =$

    (A) $\frac{4}{9}$ (B) $\frac{5}{18}$ (C) $\frac{10}{15}$ (D) $\frac{9}{36}$

17. $\frac{4}{6} - \frac{1}{4} =$

    (A) $\frac{5}{6}$ (B) $\frac{5}{8}$ (C) $\frac{3}{6}$ (D) $\frac{5}{12}$

18. $\frac{7}{12} + \frac{1}{4} =$

    (A) $\frac{5}{6}$ (B) $\frac{4}{12}$ (C) $\frac{3}{4}$ (D) $\frac{8}{12}$

Test Practice 4

Directions: Choose the decimal that equals each fraction.

1. $\frac{4}{10}$ =

   (A) 0.04 (B) 4.0 (C) 0.4 (D) 40.0

2. $\frac{18}{100}$ =

   (A) 0.018 (B) 1.8 (C) 1.08 (D) 0.18

3. $\frac{10}{10}$ =

   (A) 0.10 (B) 1.0 (C) 10.0 (D) 0.01

4. $\frac{5}{10}$ =

   (A) 5.10 (B) 0.5 (C) 0.05 (D) 5.0

5. $\frac{57}{100}$ =

   (A) 0.57 (B) 05.7 (C) 0.057 (D) 57.0

6. $\frac{8}{10}$ =

   (A) 8.0 (B) 0.81 (C) 0.08 (D) 0.8

Directions: Choose the decimal set that is in order from least to greatest.

7. (A) 0.5, 5.0, 0.05 (B) 5.0, 0.05, 0.5
   (C) 5.0, 0.5, 0.05 (D) 0.05, 0.5, 5.0

8. (A) 0.3, 0.03, 3.0 (B) 0.03, 0.3, 3.0
   (C) 0.03, 3.0, 0.3 (D) 0.3, 3.0, 0.03

9. (A) 0.43, 0.34, 0.3 (B) 0.3, 0.34, 0.43
   (C) 0.34, 0.3, 0.43 (D) 0.3, 0.43, 0.34

10. (A) 0.21, 0.19, 0.2 (B) 0.2, 0.19, 0.21
   (C) 0.19, 0.2, 0.21 (D) 0.21, 0.2, 0.19

11. (A) 0.6, 0.46, 0.64 (B) 0.46, 0.64, 0.6
   (C) 0.46, 0.6, 0.64 (D) 0.64, 0.6, 046

12. (A) 0.04, 0.41, 4.0 (B) 0.41, 4.0, 0.04
   (C) 4.0, 0.04, 0.41 (D) 0.04, 4.0, 0.41

Directions: Round each decimal to the nearest tenth.

13. 5.78

   (A) 5.7 (B) 6.0 (C) 5.9 (D) 5.8

14. 22.49

   (A) 22 (B) 22.4 (C) 22.5 (D) 23

15. 78.89

   (A) 79 (B) 78.8 (C) 78.9 (D) 7.9

16. 32.55

   (A) 32 (B) 32.6 (C) 33 (D) 32.5

17. 2.84

   (A) 2.9 (B) 2.8 (C) 3 (D) 2.0

18. 1.65

   (A) 1.7 (B) 1.6 (C) 2.0 (D) 1.5

Test Practice 5 ❧ ❧ ❧ ❧ ❧ ❧ ❧ ❧

Directions: Add or subtract the decimals in these problems.

1. 0.45 + 2.7 Ⓐ 2.15 Ⓑ 3.15 Ⓒ 2.35 Ⓓ 2.05	**2.** 7.68 − 3.79 Ⓐ 3.89 Ⓑ 3.11 Ⓒ 3.99 Ⓓ 4.89	**3.** 9.9 − 3.72 Ⓐ 6.18 Ⓑ 6.28 Ⓒ 5.18 Ⓓ 13.62
4. 16 − 6.35 Ⓐ 10.35 Ⓑ 9.35 Ⓒ 9.65 Ⓓ 22.35	**5.** 99.08 − 9.09 Ⓐ 99.99 Ⓑ 89.91 Ⓒ 89.98 Ⓓ 89.99	**6.** $22.13 − $13.40 Ⓐ $8.33 Ⓑ $8.73 Ⓒ $8.83 Ⓓ $9.73
7. 20.9 + 3.98 Ⓐ 24.98 Ⓑ 17.01 Ⓒ 24.78 Ⓓ 24.88	**8.** 6.06 + 9.66 Ⓐ 15.76 Ⓑ 15.72 Ⓒ 16.72 Ⓓ 3.63	**9.** 13 − 11.99 Ⓐ 11.86 Ⓑ 2.99 Ⓒ 1.1 Ⓓ 1.01
10. 2.1 − 1.22 Ⓐ 0.98 Ⓑ 0.8 Ⓒ 0.88 Ⓓ 1.88	**11.** $7.01 + $4.90 Ⓐ $12.01 Ⓑ $11.10 Ⓒ $11.81 Ⓓ $11.91	**12.** 101 − 1.01 Ⓐ 102.01 Ⓑ 99.99 Ⓒ 90.99 Ⓓ 100.99
13. $45.16 − $5.99 Ⓐ $51.15 Ⓑ $39.27 Ⓒ $40.17 Ⓓ $39.17	**14.** $54.04 + $33.71 Ⓐ $87.75 Ⓑ $21.67 Ⓒ $35.00 Ⓓ $87.00	

Directions: Select the closest estimated sums and differences.

15. $23.50 + $45.76 =

Ⓐ $70   Ⓑ $22   Ⓒ $72   Ⓓ $21

16. 21.7 − 12.2 =

Ⓐ 10   Ⓑ 34   Ⓒ 33   Ⓓ 9

17. $48.05 + $16.09 =

Ⓐ $65   Ⓑ $32   Ⓒ $52   Ⓓ $64

18. 103.44 − 1.34 =

Ⓐ 102   Ⓑ 104   Ⓒ 105   Ⓓ 101

19. 33.01 − 31.00 =

Ⓐ 2   Ⓑ 64   Ⓒ 3   Ⓓ 60

20. 1.18 + 201.0 =

Ⓐ 200   Ⓑ 201   Ⓒ 203   Ⓓ 202

Test Practice 6

Directions: Convert these decimals and fractions to percents.

1. 0.23

Ⓐ 2.3% Ⓑ 0.23% Ⓒ 230% Ⓓ 23%

2. 0.03

Ⓐ 3% Ⓑ 30% Ⓒ .3% Ⓓ 300%

3. 3.80

Ⓐ 38% Ⓑ 3.8% Ⓒ .38% Ⓓ 380%

4. 1.75

Ⓐ 17.55% Ⓑ 175% Ⓒ 17.5% Ⓓ 1.75%

5. 0.09

Ⓐ 9% Ⓑ 90% Ⓒ .90% Ⓓ .09%

6. 0.11

Ⓐ 11% Ⓑ 1.1% Ⓒ .11% Ⓓ 101%

7. $\frac{1}{2}$

Ⓐ 12% Ⓑ 5% Ⓒ 5.0% Ⓓ 50%

8. $\frac{1}{4}$

Ⓐ 14% Ⓑ 50% Ⓒ 25% Ⓓ 2.5%

9. $\frac{16}{100}$

Ⓐ 16% Ⓑ 1.6% Ⓒ 160% Ⓓ .16%

10. $\frac{4}{100}$

Ⓐ 40% Ⓑ 400% Ⓒ 4% Ⓓ .04%

Directions: Convert these percents to decimals.

11. 27%

Ⓐ 0.027 Ⓑ 0.27 Ⓒ 2.7 Ⓓ 2.07

12. 7%

Ⓐ .70 Ⓑ 0.07 Ⓒ 7.0 Ⓓ 70

13. 99%

Ⓐ .909 Ⓑ 0.909 Ⓒ 9.9 Ⓓ 0.99

14. 37%

Ⓐ 0.37 Ⓑ 37.0 Ⓒ 3.7 Ⓓ 0.037

Directions: Compute these percents.

15. 30% of 100 =

Ⓐ 70 Ⓑ 300 Ⓒ 3 Ⓓ 30

16. 50% of 40 =

Ⓐ 20 Ⓑ 10 Ⓒ 200 Ⓓ 2

17. 35% of 80 =

Ⓐ 28 Ⓑ 35 Ⓒ 280 Ⓓ 38

18. 25% of 60 =

Ⓐ 25 Ⓑ 30 Ⓒ 1.5 Ⓓ 15

19. 40% of 200 =

Ⓐ 40 Ⓑ 80 Ⓒ 120 Ⓓ 160

20. 30% of 50 =

Ⓐ 15 Ⓑ 30 Ⓒ 1.5 Ⓓ 35

Answer Sheet

Test Practice 1	Test Practice 2	Test Practice 3	Test Practice 4	Test Practice 5	Test Practice 6
1. Ⓐ Ⓑ Ⓒ Ⓓ	1. Ⓐ Ⓑ Ⓒ Ⓓ	1. Ⓐ Ⓑ Ⓒ Ⓓ	1. Ⓐ Ⓑ Ⓒ Ⓓ	1. Ⓐ Ⓑ Ⓒ Ⓓ	1. Ⓐ Ⓑ Ⓒ Ⓓ
2. Ⓐ Ⓑ Ⓒ Ⓓ	2. Ⓐ Ⓑ Ⓒ Ⓓ	2. Ⓐ Ⓑ Ⓒ Ⓓ	2. Ⓐ Ⓑ Ⓒ Ⓓ	2. Ⓐ Ⓑ Ⓒ Ⓓ	2. Ⓐ Ⓑ Ⓒ Ⓓ
3. Ⓐ Ⓑ Ⓒ Ⓓ	3. Ⓐ Ⓑ Ⓒ Ⓓ	3. Ⓐ Ⓑ Ⓒ Ⓓ	3. Ⓐ Ⓑ Ⓒ Ⓓ	3. Ⓐ Ⓑ Ⓒ Ⓓ	3. Ⓐ Ⓑ Ⓒ Ⓓ
4. Ⓐ Ⓑ Ⓒ Ⓓ	4. Ⓐ Ⓑ Ⓒ Ⓓ	4. Ⓐ Ⓑ Ⓒ Ⓓ	4. Ⓐ Ⓑ Ⓒ Ⓓ	4. Ⓐ Ⓑ Ⓒ Ⓓ	4. Ⓐ Ⓑ Ⓒ Ⓓ
5. Ⓐ Ⓑ Ⓒ Ⓓ	5. Ⓐ Ⓑ Ⓒ Ⓓ	5. Ⓐ Ⓑ Ⓒ Ⓓ	5. Ⓐ Ⓑ Ⓒ Ⓓ	5. Ⓐ Ⓑ Ⓒ Ⓓ	5. Ⓐ Ⓑ Ⓒ Ⓓ
6. Ⓐ Ⓑ Ⓒ Ⓓ	6. Ⓐ Ⓑ Ⓒ Ⓓ	6. Ⓐ Ⓑ Ⓒ Ⓓ	6. Ⓐ Ⓑ Ⓒ Ⓓ	6. Ⓐ Ⓑ Ⓒ Ⓓ	6. Ⓐ Ⓑ Ⓒ Ⓓ
7. Ⓐ Ⓑ Ⓒ Ⓓ	7. Ⓐ Ⓑ Ⓒ Ⓓ	7. Ⓐ Ⓑ Ⓒ Ⓓ	7. Ⓐ Ⓑ Ⓒ Ⓓ	7. Ⓐ Ⓑ Ⓒ Ⓓ	7. Ⓐ Ⓑ Ⓒ Ⓓ
8. Ⓐ Ⓑ Ⓒ Ⓓ	8. Ⓐ Ⓑ Ⓒ Ⓓ	8. Ⓐ Ⓑ Ⓒ Ⓓ	8. Ⓐ Ⓑ Ⓒ Ⓓ	8. Ⓐ Ⓑ Ⓒ Ⓓ	8. Ⓐ Ⓑ Ⓒ Ⓓ
9. Ⓐ Ⓑ Ⓒ Ⓓ	9. Ⓐ Ⓑ Ⓒ Ⓓ	9. Ⓐ Ⓑ Ⓒ Ⓓ	9. Ⓐ Ⓑ Ⓒ Ⓓ	9. Ⓐ Ⓑ Ⓒ Ⓓ	9. Ⓐ Ⓑ Ⓒ Ⓓ
10. Ⓐ Ⓑ Ⓒ Ⓓ	10. Ⓐ Ⓑ Ⓒ Ⓓ	10. Ⓐ Ⓑ Ⓒ Ⓓ	10. Ⓐ Ⓑ Ⓒ Ⓓ	10. Ⓐ Ⓑ Ⓒ Ⓓ	10. Ⓐ Ⓑ Ⓒ Ⓓ
11. Ⓐ Ⓑ Ⓒ Ⓓ	11. Ⓐ Ⓑ Ⓒ Ⓓ	11. Ⓐ Ⓑ Ⓒ Ⓓ	11. Ⓐ Ⓑ Ⓒ Ⓓ	11. Ⓐ Ⓑ Ⓒ Ⓓ	11. Ⓐ Ⓑ Ⓒ Ⓓ
12. Ⓐ Ⓑ Ⓒ Ⓓ	12. Ⓐ Ⓑ Ⓒ Ⓓ	12. Ⓐ Ⓑ Ⓒ Ⓓ	12. Ⓐ Ⓑ Ⓒ Ⓓ	12. Ⓐ Ⓑ Ⓒ Ⓓ	12. Ⓐ Ⓑ Ⓒ Ⓓ
13. Ⓐ Ⓑ Ⓒ Ⓓ	13. Ⓐ Ⓑ Ⓒ Ⓓ	13. Ⓐ Ⓑ Ⓒ Ⓓ	13. Ⓐ Ⓑ Ⓒ Ⓓ	13. Ⓐ Ⓑ Ⓒ Ⓓ	13. Ⓐ Ⓑ Ⓒ Ⓓ
14. Ⓐ Ⓑ Ⓒ Ⓓ	14. Ⓐ Ⓑ Ⓒ Ⓓ	14. Ⓐ Ⓑ Ⓒ Ⓓ	14. Ⓐ Ⓑ Ⓒ Ⓓ	14. Ⓐ Ⓑ Ⓒ Ⓓ	14. Ⓐ Ⓑ Ⓒ Ⓓ
15. Ⓐ Ⓑ Ⓒ Ⓓ	15. Ⓐ Ⓑ Ⓒ Ⓓ	15. Ⓐ Ⓑ Ⓒ Ⓓ	15. Ⓐ Ⓑ Ⓒ Ⓓ	15. Ⓐ Ⓑ Ⓒ Ⓓ	15. Ⓐ Ⓑ Ⓒ Ⓓ
16. Ⓐ Ⓑ Ⓒ Ⓓ	16. Ⓐ Ⓑ Ⓒ Ⓓ	16. Ⓐ Ⓑ Ⓒ Ⓓ	16. Ⓐ Ⓑ Ⓒ Ⓓ	16. Ⓐ Ⓑ Ⓒ Ⓓ	16. Ⓐ Ⓑ Ⓒ Ⓓ
17. Ⓐ Ⓑ Ⓒ Ⓓ	17. Ⓐ Ⓑ Ⓒ Ⓓ	17. Ⓐ Ⓑ Ⓒ Ⓓ	17. Ⓐ Ⓑ Ⓒ Ⓓ	17. Ⓐ Ⓑ Ⓒ Ⓓ	17. Ⓐ Ⓑ Ⓒ Ⓓ
18. Ⓐ Ⓑ Ⓒ Ⓓ	18. Ⓐ Ⓑ Ⓒ Ⓓ	18. Ⓐ Ⓑ Ⓒ Ⓓ	18. Ⓐ Ⓑ Ⓒ Ⓓ	18. Ⓐ Ⓑ Ⓒ Ⓓ	18. Ⓐ Ⓑ Ⓒ Ⓓ
19. Ⓐ Ⓑ Ⓒ Ⓓ	19. Ⓐ Ⓑ Ⓒ Ⓓ			19. Ⓐ Ⓑ Ⓒ Ⓓ	19. Ⓐ Ⓑ Ⓒ Ⓓ
20. Ⓐ Ⓑ Ⓒ Ⓓ	20. Ⓐ Ⓑ Ⓒ Ⓓ			20. Ⓐ Ⓑ Ⓒ Ⓓ	20. Ⓐ Ⓑ Ⓒ Ⓓ

Answer Key

Practice 1
1. 1
2. 3
3. 5
4. 8
5. 6
6. 7
7. 9
8. 7
9. 12
10. 5
11. 16
12. 8
13. 7
14. 13
15. 13
16. 10
17. shade 2
18. shade 4
19. shade 7
20. shade 1
21. shade 1
22. shade 3
23. shade 5
24. shade 8
25. shade 1
26. shade 4
27. shade 5
28. shade 3

Practice 2
1. 2
2. 6
3. 3
4. 2
5. 4
6. 10
7. 1/2
8. 1/6
9. 3/4
10. 1/3
11. 3/8
12. 7/8
13. 4/5
14. 1/4
15. 5/9
16. 3/8
17. 4/10
18. 1/3
19. shade 1/3
20. shade 4/5
21. shade 4/9
22. shade 4/6
23. shade 7/10
24. shade 5/8

Practice 3
1. 2/4
2. 2/6
3. 2/8
4. 3/9
5. 4/8
6. 2/10
7. 6/8
8. 6/12
9. 4/6
10. 3/12
11. 5/10
12. 6/9
13. 4/6
14. 6/8
15. 1/4
16. 3/4
17. 8/12
18. 4/5

Practice 4
1. 4/8
2. 2/8
3. 2/4
4. 2/6
5. 4/6
6. 2/10
7. 4/8
8. 6/8
9. 4/10
10. 2/4
11. 1/2
12. 1/3
13. 4/4
14. 6/6
15. 10/10
16. 8/10
17. 6/10
18. 3/4
19. 2/3
20. 3/4
21. 4/5
22. 5/10
23. 3/6
24. 2/4
25. 8/8

Practice 5
1. 12/8
2. 10/8
3. 4/8
4. 8/6
5. 10/6
6. 2/3
7. 8/8
8. 6/6
9. 4/4
10. 5/4
11. 8/4
12. 4/2
13. 16/8
14. 6/8
15. 1/3
16. 6/6
17. 9/6
18. 7/4
19. 4/3
20. 5/4
21. 12/6
22. 12/6
23. 8/4
24. 14/8
25. 1/4

Practice 6
1. <
2. >
3. >
4. =
5. >
6. <
7. <
8. >
9. >
10. <
11. >
12. >
13. =
14. <
15. >
16. <
17. =
18. <
19. <
20. <
21. <
22. >
23. <
24. =
25. <
26. >
27. <
28. <
29. >
30. <

Practice 7
1. 1/3
2. 2/3
3. 4/5
4. 3/4
5. 3/4
6. 1/2
7. 2/3
8. 1/4
9. 1/3
10. 1/3
11. 2/5
12. 3/5
13. 4/5
14. 3/4
15. 2/3
16. 6/7
17. 3/4
18. 7/8
19. 3/7
20. 4/5
21. 2/5
22. 1/2
23. 1/3
24. 2/3
25. 5/7
26. 2/3
27. 2/11

Practice 8
1. 9/10
2. 7/9
3. 11/12
4. 5/6
5. 3/5
6. 2/3
7. 8/9
8. 5/7
9. 5/6
10. 4/6 = 2/3
11. 2/2 = 1
12. 6/6 = 1
13. 9/10
14. 5/5 = 1
15. 10/12 = 5/6
16. 3/9 = 1/3
17. 7/7 = 1
18. 10/11
19. 10/11
20. 11/12
21. 18/20= 9/10
22. 13/15
23. 9/9 = 1
24. 9/9 = 1
25. 4/4 = 1
26. 8/11
27. 5/5 = 1
28. 3/6 = 1/2
29. 6/9 = 2/3
30. 9/12 =3/4

Practice 9
1. 4/9
2. 2/8 = 1/4
3. 2/7
4. 1/6
5. 2/5
6. 4/7
7. 1/9
8. 1/8
9. 6/12 = 1/2
10. 2/9
11. 3/15 = 1/5
12. 2/13
13. 3/10
14. 1/6
15. 3/12 = 1/4
16. 4/7
17. 6/9 = 2/3
18. 6/15 = 2/5
19. 3/10
20. 4/12 = 1/3
21. 10/16 = 5/8
22. 5/10 = 1/2
23. 3/9 = 1/3
24. 4/8 = 1/2
25. 3/11
26. 2/12 = 1/6
27. 3/15 = 1/5

Practice 10
1. proper
2. improper
3. mixed
4. proper
5. improper
6. mixed
7. proper
8. proper
9. improper
10. improper
11. proper
12. mixed
13. improper
14. improper
15. improper
16. mixed
17. improper
18. improper
19. mixed
20. improper
21. proper
22. mixed
23. improper
24. proper
25. proper
26. improper
27. improper
28. mixed
29. mixed
30. improper
31. mixed
32. improper

Practice 11
1. 1 4/5
2. 1 1/2
3. 1 2/3
4. 3 1/2
5. 2 1/3
6. 1 2/7
7. 1 5/7
8. 3 1/3
9. 2 4/5
10. 1 3/10
11. 1 3/4
12. 2 3/4
13. 1 7/9
14. 1 1/11
15. 1 1/8
16. 2 2/6 =2 1/3
17. 3 1/5
18. 4 1/5
19. 3 1/8
20. 1 6/7
21. 2 6/9 = 2 2/3
22. 2 1/4
23. 2 1/6
24. 4 2/4 = 4 1/2
25. 4 1/4
26. 2 7/10
27. 2 2/5
28. 1 2/9
29. 1 4/11
30. 2 14/15
31. 4 1/2
32. 4 1/6
33. 3 2/5

Practice 12
1. 17/7
2. 7/2
3. 17/3
4. 11/2
5. 8/3
6. 13/3
7. 9/7
8. 4/3
9. 11/7
10. 11/8
11. 5/4
12. 18/5
13. 11/5
14. 9/7
15. 35/8
16. 10/8
17. 13/5
18. 11/4
19. 23/8
20. 15/11
21. 21/9
22. 10/3
23. 25/6
24. 21/4
25. 20/6
26. 21/10
27. 20/11
28. 27/8
29. 23/6
30. 41/10

Practice 13
1. 4 2/4 = 4 1/2
2. 2 2/3
3. 5 1/5
4. 2 1/6
5. 3 1/4
6. 11 11/12
7. 7 4/6 = 7 2/3
8. 3 1/10
9. 1 1/5
10. 4 1/6
11. 3 1/3
12. 3 2/4 = 3 1/2
13. 8 4/6 = 8 2/3
14. 15 3/3 = 16
15. 1
16. 6 10/10 = 7
17. 3
18. 5 12/12 = 6
19. 7 13/13 = 8
20. 6 4/4 = 7
21. 6 3/8
22. 3
23. 7 8/8 = 8
24. 5 1/4
25. 7 1/7

Practice 14
1. 4/6, 3/6
2. 15/20, 16/20
3. 7/14, 2/14
4. 12/15, 15/15
5. 6/12, 3/12
6. 15/24, 8/24
7. 28/35, 5/35
8. 8/12, 3/12
9. 3/21, 14/21
10. 2/6, 3/6
11. 4/20, 10/20
12. 6/30, 5/30
13. 3/24, 8/24
14. 21/28, 4/28
15. 7/42, 12/42
16. 4/36, 18/36
17. 27/45, 15/45
18. 2/20, 5/20

Practice 15
1. >
2. <
3. <
4. =
5. >
6. =
7. >
8. <
9. <
10. <
11. =
12. >
13. <
14. <
15. =
16 <
17. <
18. =

Practice 16
1. 4/12, 1/2, 3/4
2. 5/12, 1/2, 4/6
3. 2/6, 1/2, 2/3
4. 1/2, 2/3, 5/6
5. 2/6, 1/2, 7/12
6. 1/6, 4/12, 1/2
7. 1/6, 2/8, 1/2
8. 1/4, 3/6, 8/12
9. 1/2, 2/3, 5/6
10. 1/6, 1/3, 1/2
11. 1/3, 5/12, 1/2
12. 3/8, 6/12, 2/3
13. 1/8, 1/4, 1/3
14. 2/6, 2/4, 2/3
15. 4/8, 4/6, 3/4
16. 3/4, 10/12, 7/8
17. 1/12, 1/8, 1/6
18. 1/2, 5/8, 9/12
19. 1/4, 3/6, 9/12
20. 5/12, 5/8, 5/6
21. 4/6, 3/4, 10/12
22. 1/6, 3/12, 3/4
23. 1/2, 5/8, 5/6
24. 3/4 5/6, 11/12
25. 2/12, 1/2, 6/8

Practice 17
1. 12
2. 8
3. 33
4. 12
5. 20
6. 6
7. 24
8. 24
9. 56
10. 14
11. 30
12. 24
13. 20
14. 60
15. 9
16. 18
17. 40
18. 14

Practice 18
1. 3/12 = 1/4
2. 11/24
3. 10/12 = 5/6
4. 2/10 = 1/5
5. 7/24
6. 5/6
7. 7/18
8. 7/12
9. 13/12 = 1 1/12
10. 17/15 = 1 2/15
11. 1/9
12. 3/20
13. 7/10
14. 7/12
15. 29/24 = 1 5/24

Practice 19
1. 20/100 = 0.20 or 0.2
2. 25/100 = 0.25
3. 6/100 = 0.06
4. 44/100 = 0.44
5. 82/100 = 0.82
6. 16/100 = 0.16
7. 92/100 = 0.92
8. 28/100 = 0.28
9. 19/100 = 0.19
10. 35/100 = 0.35
11. 3/100 = 0.03
12. 65/100 = 0.65
13. 39/100 = 0.39
14. 11/100 = 0.11
15. 99/100 = 0.99
16. 30 squares shaded
17. 60 squares shaded
18. 10 squares shaded
19. 31 squares shaded
20. 65 squares shaded
21. 92 squares shaded

Practice 20
1. 0.4
2. 0.61
3. 0.5
4. 0.7
5. 0.73
6. 0.31
7. 1.0 or 1
8. 0.9
9. 0.88
10. 0.44
11. 0.69
12. 0.09
13. 0.07
14. 0.18
15. 0.03
16. 4/10 = 2/5
17. 5/100 = 1/20
18. 18/100 = 9/50
19. 13/100
20. 23/100
21. 47/100
22. 9/100
23. 1/100
24. 10/100 = 1/10
25. 57/100
26. 78/100 = 39/50
27. 20/100 = 2/10 = 1/5
28. 8/10 = 4/5
29. 8/100 = 2/25
30. 99/100

Practice 21
1. 0.3
2. 0.25
3. 0.5
4. 0.7
5. 0.8
6. 0.9
7. 1.0 or 1
8. 0.6
9. 0.6
10. 0.2
11. 0.4
16. 25/100 = 1/4
17. 4/10 = 2/5
18. 6/10 = 3/5
19. 5/10 = 1/2
20. 7/10
21. 2/10 = 1/5
22. 3/10
23. 9/10
24. 1/10
25. 75/100 = 3/4
26. 8/10 = 4/5

Answer Key

12. 0.75
13. 1.0 or 1
14. 0.5
15. 0.8

27. 1/1 = 1
28. 0.2
29. 0.5
30. 1/4

Practice 22
1. 1.5, 1 50/100 = 1 1/2
2. 1.32, 1 32/100 = 1 8/25
3. 2.39, 2 39/100
4. 2.61, 2 61/100
5. 1.13, 1 13/100
6. 2.98, 2 98/100 = 2 49/50
7. 1.75
8. 1.6
9. 1.2
10. 2.5
11. 4.3
12. 5.41
13. 7.1
14. 2.06
15. 1.31
16. 1.07
17. 5.91
18. 3.09
19. 4.22
20. 1.03
21. 2.25

Practice 23
1. <
2. >
3. <
4. <
5. >
6. >
7. <
8. =
9. <
10. >
11. >

12. <
13. >
14. >
15. =
16. <
17. >
18. >
19. <
20. >
21. =
22. >

23. <
24. >
25. >
26. <
27. <
28. >
29. <
30. >
31. =
32. >
33. <

Practice 24
1. 0.05, 0.25, 0.5
2. 0.50, 0.75, 0.85
3. 0.20, 0.40, 0.65
4. 0.08, 0.8, 0.81
5. 0.53, 0.6, 0.63
6. 0.04, 0.40, 0.44
7. 0.09, 0.69, 0.96
8. 0.05, 0.35, 0.53
9. 0.89, 0.9, 0.91
10. 0.12, 0.2, 0.21
11. 0.04, 0.46, 0.5
12. 0.09, 0.89, 0.9

13. 0.12, 0.21, 2.1
14. 0.04, 3.63, 4.6
15. 0.06, 0.65, 5.6
16. 0.3, 0.34, 3.03
17. 0.08, 0.8, 8.0
18. 0.05, 3.05, 5.01
19. 0.5, 5.18, 5.81
20. 0.3, 0.31, 3.18
21. 0.01, 0.1, 1.0
22. 2.4, 2.42, 4.02
23. 0.55, 5.05, 5.5
24. 1.24, 2.14, 2.41

Practice 25
1. 5
2. 8
3. 1
4. 8
5. 8
6. 5
7. 9
8. 4
9. 4
10. 7
11. 3
12. 4

13. 2
14. 2
15. 7
16. 0.5
17. 2.4
18. 0.8
19. 3.9
20. 3.0
21. 0.9
22. 1.8
23. 0.2
24. 0.6

25. 0.6
26. 3.9
27. 0.4
28. 0.1
29. 5.6
30. 4.5
31. 2.5
32. 10.0
33. 6.1
34. 79.8
35. 27.8
36. 1.0

Practice 26
1. 9.42
2. 6.26
3. 9.33
4. 5.91
5. 9.00
6. 21.01
7. 7.76
8. 2.88
9. 52.01
10. 10.00
11. 13.26
12. 40.09
13. 29.7
14. 7.01

15. 58.16
16. 1.37
17. 43.01
18. 4.11
19. 72.77
20. 109.01
21. 1.21
22. 22.32
23. 10.89
24. 6.66
25. 9.3
26. 16.3
27. 20.01

Practice 27
1. 4.86
2. 0.03
3. 0.61
4. 58.83
5. 4.07
6. 3.78
7. 0.01
8. 18.11
9. 1.19

10. 13.89
11. 2.09
12. 0.11
13. 2.2
14. 3.1
15. 1.01
16. 0.99
17. 0.01
18. 0.03

19. 1.02
20. 0.8
21. 2.23
22. 1.98
23. 0.18
24. 99.99
25. 0.22
26. 0.89
27. 29.97

Practice 28
1. 4 − 2 = 2
2. 8 + 3 = 11
3. 2 − 2 = 0
4. 9 + 6 = 15
5. 8 − 5 = 3
6. 8 + 8 = 16
7. 8 − 4 = 4
8. 7 + 9 = 16
9. 9 − 9 = 0
10. 3 − 3 = 0
11. 6 + 6 = 12
12. 14 + 6 = 20

13. 67 − 7 = 60
14. 17 − 8 = 9
15. 23 + 2 = 25
16. 9 − 4 = 5
17. 28 − 28 = 0
18. 4 + 40 = 44
19. 7 + 67 = 74
20. 40 − 21 = 19
21. 23 + 3 = 26
22. 9 − 9 = 0
23. 100 − 1 = 99
24. 99 − 99 = 0

Practice 29
1. $6.05
2. $1.83
3. $14.02
4. $3.77
5. $12.59
6. $3.89
7. $2.91
8. $30.00
9. $5.89
10. $21.69
11. $28.75
12. $132.01
13. $77.28
14. $44.02

15. $10.30
16. $0.11
17. $99.34
18. $824.43
19. $21.03
20. $83.34
21. $2.10
22. $0.05
23. $101.00
24. $91.01
25. $188.87
26. $76.11
27. $2.34

Practice 30
1. 30%
2. 9%
3. 51%
4. 88%
5. 13%
6. 38%
7. 11%
8. 22%

9. 7%
10. 93%
11. 14%
12. 3%
13. 64%
14. 24%
15. 75%

Practice 31
Shade in:
1. 32%
2. 45%
3. 78%
4. 99%
5. 12%
6. 4%

7. 50%
8. 29%
9. 66%
10. 19%
11. 6%
12. 85%

13. 40%
14. 80%
15. 33%
16. 2%
17. 92%
18. 100%

Practice 32
1. 20%
2. 19%
3. 34%
4. 57%
5. 50%
6. 1%
7. 3%
8. 80%
9. 11%
10. 14%
11. 99%
12. 67%

13. 78%
14. 86%
15. 61%
16. 13%
17. 30%
18. 50%
19. 10%
20. 77%
21. 7%
22. 6%
23. 41%
24. 4%

25. 75%
26. 9%
27. 90%
28. 2%
29. 60%
30. 0%
31. 37%
32. 88%
33. 26%
34. 18%
35. 23%
36. 47%

Practice 33
1. 0.4
2. 0.03
3. 0.33
4. 0.5
5. 0.66
6. 0.99
7. 0.91
8. 0.54
9. 0.8
10. 0.61
11. 0.12
12. 0.04
13. 0.21
14. 0.09
15. 0.18
16. 0.02
17. 0.69

18. 0.19
19. 2.31
20. 1.56
21. 1.01
22. 1.11
23. 2.99
24. 2.09
25. 1.40 or 1.4
26. 1.55
27. 1.10 or 1.1
28. 3.0
29. 0.3
30. 0.03
31. 0.6
32. 0.06
33. 1.06

Practice 34
1. 50/100 = 1/2
2. 25/100 = 1/4
3. 19/100
4. 6/100 = 3/50
5. 90/100 = 9/10
6. 40/100 = 4/10 = 2/5
7. 22/100 = 11/50
8. 16/100 = 4/25
9. 31/100
10. 70/100 = 7/10
11. 66/100 = 33/50
12. 37/100
13. 91/100
14. 12/100 = 3/25
15. 3/100
16. 25%
17. 20%

18. 30%
19. 50%
20. 70%
21. 50%
22. 90%
23. 71%
24. 38%
25. 40%
26. 75%
27. 80%
28. 33%
29. 60%
30. 27%
31. 4%
32. 3%
33. 80%

Practice 35
1. 250%
2. 175%
3. 217%
4. 551%
5. 150%
6. 319%
7. 199%
8. 450%

18. 108%
19. 321%
20. 550%
21. 325%
22. 598%
23. 601%
24. 824%
25. 133%

9. 350%
10. 220%
11. 701%
12. 303%
13. 400%
14. 625%
15. 520%
16. 180%
17. 180%

26. 333%
27. 210%
28. 330%
29. 523%
30. 270%
31. 120%
32. 416%
33. 179%

Practice 36
1. 15
2. 9.6
3. 34
4. 11.6
5. 8.1
6. 35
7. 80
8. 24
9. 20

10. 7.2
11. 12
12. 60
13. 4.84
14. 15
15. 6
16. 35.2
17. 21.6
18. 11

Test Practice 1
1. C
2. B
3. C
4. A
5. C
6. A
7. A

8. A
9. A
10. B
11. D
12. B
13. D
14. A

15. C
16. C
17. B
18. B
19. C
20. B

Test Practice 2
1. C
2. A
3. D
4. C
5. A
6. D
7. C

8. D
9. B
10. D
11. B
12. C
13. B
14. D

15. A
16. D
17. D
18. B
19. B
20. D

Test Practice 3
1. C
2. D
3. B
4. B
5. B
6. D

7. C
8. D
9. D
10. B
11. C
12. A

13. D
14. D
15. A
16. B
17. D
18. A

Test Practice 4
1. C
2. D
3. B
4. B
5. A
6. D

7. D
8. B
9. B
10. C
11. C
12. A

13. D
14. C
15. C
16. B
17. B
18. A

Test Practice 5
1. B
2. A
3. A
4. C
5. D
6. B
7. D

8. B
9. D
10. C
11. D
12. B
13. D
14. A

15. A
16. A
17. D
18. A
19. A
20. D

Test Practice 6
1. D
2. A
3. D
4. B
5. A
6. A
7. D

8. C
9. A
10. C
11. B
12. B
13. D
14. A

15. D
16. A
17. A
18. D
19. B
20. A